Written By Michael Bridge

A Grange Publication

ISBN 978-1-906211-46-2

£6.99

CONTENTS

PUMA
MANSION.COM CASINO & POKER
TOTTENHAM HOTSPUR
www.superleaguefo

WELCOME

Welcome to the 2009 Official Tottenham Hotspur Annual.

The 2007/2008 campaign was certainly an eventful season. Our memorable Carling Cup victory will be remembered by Spurs fans young and old. During this thrilling cup-run, Spurs convincingly disposed of North London rivals Arsenal before triumphing over West London rivals Chelsea at Wembley. This was the first major trophy for the club in nine years, and fittingly fell alongside the club's 125th Anniversary.

There is also much to look forward to in the new season. Juande Ramos enters his first full campaign in charge and expectations for Spurs are high. A vibrant mix of firm fan favourites such as Ledley King and Michael Dawson combined with new blood in the likes of Luka Modric, Giovani dos Santos and David Bentley certainly makes for an exciting season.

In the following pages, you will find a comprehensive 2007/2008 season review and an in-depth look into the new Ramos regime. Player profiles, along with a quiz section and a fascinating 'Did you know' page will leave you with a wealth of Spurs knowledge which is bound to impress your friends.

So enjoy the Tottenham Hotspur 2009 Annual . . . Come on you Spurs!

Michael Bridge.

CARLING CUP

Tottenham Hotspur saved their best performances for the 2007/2008 Carling Cup. Impressive victories at Manchester City and at home to great rivals Arsenal culminated in our first final at the new Wembley Stadium. Coming from a goal behind, goals from Dimitar Berbatov and Jonathan Woodgate ensured a fourth League Cup triumph.

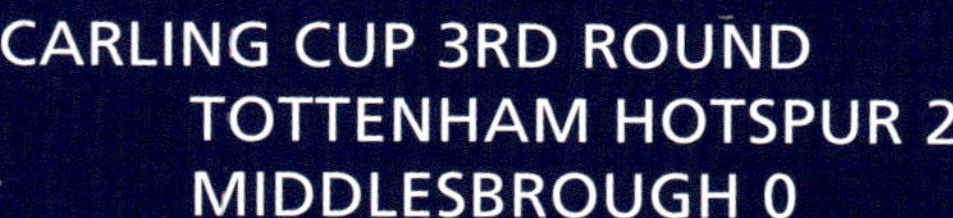

CARLING CUP 3RD ROUND
TOTTENHAM HOTSPUR 2
MIDDLESBROUGH 0

Spurs' 2-0 victory against the 2004 Winners Middlesbrough kicked off the 2007/2008 Carling Cup run. Both clubs fielded strong sides, and this produced a tight and entertaining game. Gareth Bale put Spurs ahead in the 72nd minute, with his third strike in five appearances. Robbie Keane's good work near the touchline in our own half found Bale who rounded Middlesbrough goalkeeper Brad Jones to give Spurs the lead. Three minutes later, Spurs booked a place in the fourth round. Paul Robinson sent a big clearance straight to Aaron Lennon and his cross was met by a Tom Huddlestone header to make the game secure. It was a strong home performance by Spurs, with Bale playing a starring role.

CARLING CUP 4TH ROUND
TOTTENHAM HOTSPUR 2
BLACKPOOL 0

New Head Coach Juande Ramos got off to a winning start over a stubborn Blackpool side. Ramos picked his strongest available team in what was far from a stroll on a mild night in October. It was a route-one goal starting with Paul Robinson that put Spurs ahead. Dimitar Berbatov nodded on the high kick and Robbie Keane flicked the ball over the Blackpool goalkeeper. Blackpool didn't get despondent and to their credit they had numerous chances to equalize, but Spurs' passage through to the Quarter Final was confirmed when a Steed Malbranque corner found Pascal Chimbonda at the back post. His powerful header gave us the victory in what was a solid start for Ramos in a potential 'banana skin'.

CARLING CUP 5TH ROUND
MANCHESTER CITY 0
TOTTENHAM HOTSPUR 2

Spurs produced one of their best performances of the season with this fantastic win over an in-form Manchester City, who were undefeated at home in all competitions. Spurs combined scintillating attacks with solid defending in order to book a place in the Semi Final. Aaron Lennon's good work on the wing found Jermain Defoe with ease, giving Spurs the lead at the City of Manchester Stadium. Substitute Jamie O'Hara made a significant impression on the game at a time when City continued to pressurise Spurs. O'Hara's long ball found Steed Malbranque, who passed Richard Dunne, scoring a fine goal beyond the reach of City's Joe Hart. Playing with ten men for 70 minutes, Spurs defended with pride and attacked with purpose to set up a Semi Final re-match with Arsenal.

CARLING CUP SEMI FINAL FIRST LEG
ARSENAL 1
TOTTENHAM HOTSPUR 1

Spurs returned to the Emirates Stadium only a few weeks after a narrow Premier League defeat to Arsenal. This meeting was the second time in successive seasons where one of the Carling Cup Semi Finals was also a North London derby. After an entertaining start Spurs started to create the better chances yet were unable to open the scoring. Arsenal struggled to threaten the Spurs goal with Ledley King easily disposing of anything that came near him. Spurs continued to dominate

and the hard work finally paid off when Robbie Keane found Jermaine Jenas in the box. Jenas finished with ease to the delight of the vocal travelling support. The second half saw Spurs continue to press for a second goal as the home side were becoming frustrated. They were allowed a route back into the game after a Theo Walcott effort took a huge deflection off Lee Young-Pyo to somehow find its way into the goal. We left the Emirates disappointed after such a dominant display but this result left the second leg wide open, with everything to play for.

CARLING CUP SEMI FINAL SECOND LEG TOTTENHAM HOTSPUR 5 ARSENAL 1

There have been many memorable nights at White Hart Lane over the years and it's fair to say January 22 2008 will be up there with the very best as Spurs annihilated rivals Arsenal.

Our date at Wembley on February 24 was confirmed after a 6-2 aggregate win over Arsenal. The atmosphere prior to the match had the usual deafening noise coming from all corners of the ground. Spurs set out to attack from the first minute and Jermaine Jenas put the home side in front after a wonderful run beat all of the Arsenal midfield and defence to make it 2-1 on aggregate. A Nicklas Bendtner own goal increased the lead to put Spurs 2-0 ahead at half-time. There was understandable anxiety around the stadium at the break, having not beaten Arsenal since 1999 and thinking back to the countless occasions Spurs have taken the lead yet failed to maintain the advantage. However, it proved to be the night of the Lilywhites after Robbie Keane made it 3-0 to Spurs soon after half-time. With fingernails still being bitten inside the ground, Aaron Lennon all-but confirmed our place in the Final with a cool finish to make it 4-0 to Spurs.

It was fast becoming a 'glory glory' night for Tottenham Hotspur. Emmanuel Adebayor pulled a goal back for Arsenal with an unstoppable strike past Radek Cerny, yet Spurs were destined to have the final say when a tireless Jenas raced into the box passing Arsenal's Gilberto with ease to find Steed Malbranque who made it 5-1 to Spurs. The players embraced at the final whistle, they congratulated themselves on a wonderful performance and a dominant display over two legs. Arsenal were defeated, out-played at home and away. Any post-match talk of Spurs having only beaten the Arsenal 'kids' was foolish, with

key players such as captain Gallas, Fabregas, Gilberto, Hleb and Sagna all featuring in the line-up. Let there be no doubt, Spurs had waited too long for this moment and the feeling of beating the old enemy was palpable throughout this match.

CARLING CUP FINAL
TOTTENHAM HOTSPUR 2 CHELSEA 1

(AET – Score 1-1 after 90 minutes)
Attendance: 87,660

Spurs (4-4-2):- Robinson; Hutton, Woodgate, King (Capt.), Chimbonda (sub Huddlestone, 62); Lennon, Jenas, Zokora, Malbranque (sub Tainio, 75); Berbatov, Keane (sub Kaboul, 102)
Subs not used:- Cerny; Bent

Chelsea (4-1-3-2):- Cech; Belletti, Carvalho, Terry (Capt.), Bridge; Mikel (sub Cole, 99); Wright-Phillips (sub Kalou, 72), Essien (sub Ballack, 88), Lampard; Drogba, Anelka
Subs not used:- Cudicini; Alex

An outstanding performance saw Spurs come from a goal behind to win the League Cup for the fourth time after beating Chelsea in extra-time. Tottenham were by far the better side on the day. The determination by every single player ensured that there would only be one outcome at the end of the match – a victory for Tottenham Hotspur which guaranteed European football for a third successive season

Spurs were on the attack from the first minute after Robbie Keane pounced on a mistake by Juliano Belletti to hit a shot which was deflected out for a corner. This set the stage for Spurs to dominate as they had done in the Semi Final. Dimitar Berbatov, Jonathan Woodgate and Steed Malbranque all came close to bringing Spurs the lead as Chelsea failed to produce any clear-cut chances. However, when Spurs conceded a free-kick in a dangerous area, Didier Drogba's curled effort gave Chelsea the lead against the run of play. The goal advantage did little to liven up the Chelsea fans who remained largely anonymous

in comparison to the vocal Tottenham support. After the break, Juande Ramos substituted Pascal Chimbonda for Tom Huddlestone, which proved to be a masterstroke. Aaron Lennon was moved to the left-wing with Jermaine Jenas now playing behind the strikers, making Spurs a strong, attacking unit. A hand-ball by Wayne Bridge gave Spurs a penalty kick. Berbatov has since claimed he was nervous before taking this penalty, yet he looked like the coolest person in the 90,000 seater stadium as he confidently strode to the penalty spot, scoring the equaliser with style. Spurs were on level terms, and deservedly so. Chelsea were not given time to regroup as Spurs continued to attack, striving to find the winning goal. With the supporters starting to clock-watch, Didier Zokora somehow found himself one-on-one with Petr Cech. His first effort was saved and he put the rebound agonisingly wide. The Spurs strikers continued to threaten, but the game finished level on 90 minutes. Spurs clearly had the ascendancy going into extra-time and the dramatic winning goal came following a Spurs free-kick. Jenas launched his kick into the box, Woodgate headed the ball against Cech's fist and the ball rebounded back off Woodgate's head and into the net to put Spurs in front. Chelsea pressed for an equaliser but the whole Spurs side stood firm against their attacks, defending in numbers. Woodgate and Ledley King were simply immense at the back and Jenas must take great credit for his unstoppable running even after 120 minutes. The final whistle came and the celebrations began. Spurs had won the 2008 Carling Cup. Keane was overcome with emotion and the most passionate fans in the country found themselves minutes away from watching the side lift the trophy. King became the latest in a line of great captains to lift silverware for Spurs. It was fitting to see Keane, stand-in captain in the frequent absence through injury of King, lift the cup alongside the skipper. This also meant that Ramos remained unbeaten in all cup finals as a manager after five triumphs with Sevilla. The day belonged to Tottenham Hotspur, and it was a day never to be forgotten.

PREMIER LEAGUE REVIEW 2007/2008

The 2007/2008 season was a disappointing league campaign. After two consecutive 5th place league finishes, hopes were high in August 2007. A poor start resulted in the exit of both Martin Jol and Chris Hughton and the arrival of Juande Ramos, Marcos Alvarez and Gus Poyet in October. A steady rise from 18th in November to 11th by May reflected the level of improvement experienced at the club.

AUGUST

Pld: 4 W: 1 D: 0 L: 3

A newly-promoted Sunderland under the charge of Roy Keane were Spurs' first opponents. As the game looked to be a certain draw, Michael Chopra scored in the dying minutes of the match, forcing Spurs to return to the Lane pointless. The first home game also ended in defeat to Everton, Anthony Gardner being the sole goalscorer in a disappointing 3-1 defeat. Spurs' first points of the season came at home against Derby. The game began in blistering fashion as a Jermaine Jenas goal, and a Steed Malbranque double gave Spurs a comfortable 3-0 lead after only 14 minutes. Darren Bent scored his first league goal for Spurs to wrap-up a 4-0 win. The final game in an eventful August was a trip to Old Trafford. Gareth Bale was outstanding on his debut as Spurs went down to a narrow 1-0 defeat when a point was the least they deserved.

SEPTEMBER

Pld: 3 W: 0 D: 2 L: 1

Spurs endured further frustrations at Craven Cottage with a 3-3 draw against Fulham. Gareth Bale looked to have won the game; however, a horrible deflection off Ricardo Rocha gave Fulham a glimmer of hope and in injury-time, Diomansy Kamara's overhead kick gave Fulham their equaliser, denying Spurs their first away win of the season. The first North London derby of the season ended in disappointment as Arsenal recorded a 3-1 win. Robbie Keane was our goalscorer in the 1-1 draw away to Bolton.

OCTOBER

Pld: 4 W: 0 D: 2 L: 2

Aston Villa were the visitors on a memorable night marking the club's 125th Anniversary. Trailing 4-1 Spurs produced an amazing fightback with Younes Kaboul scoring a late equaliser to make it 4-4. Two Robbie Keane goals at Liverpool looked to be enough to secure a 2-1 victory until a very late Fernando Torres strike saw Spurs drop two vital points. A 3-1 defeat away to Newcastle left Spurs in the relegation zone in Martin Jol's final league match in charge. Under the temporary management of Clive Allen, Spurs were dealt the agony of another injury-time goal against Blackburn, losing 2-1.

NOVEMBER

Pld: 3 W: 1 D: 2 L: 0

Juande Ramos' first league match in charge resulted in a 1-1 draw with Middlesbrough at the Riverside Stadium. A much-needed win was secured against Wigan in our next fixture. Two goals from Jermaine Jenas and one from Aaron Lennon gave Spurs a 3-0 lead by half time. Darren Bent completed the scoring with a late goal in a 4-0 win to lift Spurs to 14th, and away from trouble. One point was secured at Upton Park but Spurs left the ground frustrated as Jermain Defoe missed his injury-time penalty, much to the relief of West Ham's Robert Green.

DECEMBER

Pld: 6 W: 4 D: 0 L: 2

Juande Ramos suffered his first defeat in charge after a 3-2 defeat at home to Birmingham. Yet another late goal won the game for Birmingham in a match where Spurs dominated. Robbie Keane's highly debatable red card proved to be the talking point as the fans left the ground in disbelief. Superior possession finally turned to points as an in-form Manchester City were beaten 2-1 with a late Jermain Defoe goal. December was turning out to be a fine month, with Dimitar Berbatov scoring the winner at Portsmouth. A much-depleted squad travelled to the Emirates and were unfortunate to go down to a 2-1 defeat. Christmas, however, was a great time to be a Spurs fan. The 5-1 win over Fulham on Boxing Day was a treat to watch while an added bonus to the scoreline was the return of Ledley King. A breathtaking 10-goal extravaganza took place at the Lane three days later as four goals from Berbatov sealed an incredible 6-4 win and another three precious points against Reading.

JANUARY
Pld: 4 W: 1 D: 1 L: 2

The trip to Aston Villa on New Year's Day ended in disappointment as a late Martin Laursen header ensured the points stayed at Villa Park. Between FA and Carling Cup matches Spurs travelled to Chelsea in the League but suffered a 2-0 defeat in what was an extremely busy month of league and cup football. Spurs returned to winning ways in the league with a 2-0 win at home to Sunderland. A well-earned point was achieved at Everton with Jonathan Woodgate making his Spurs debut.

FEBRUARY
Pld: 2 W: 1 D: 1 L: 0

Spurs were seconds away from a triumphant and well-deserved home victory over champions Manchester United in early February. However, a last-minute Carlos Tevez goal from a corner cancelled out Dimitar Berbatov's first-half opener. The good form continued as Spurs eased to a 3-0 win over Derby County. Second-half goals from Robbie Keane, Younes Kaboul and Berbatov sent Spurs home with three away points.

MARCH
Pld: 6 W: 2 D: 1 L: 3

Six days after lifting the Carling Cup, Spurs suffered a disappointing 4-1 defeat to Birmingham. A Jermaine Jenas goal was the only consolation to take from this match. The best league performance of the season came at home to London rivals West Ham, with a 4-0 victory. Two Dimitar Berbatov headers gave Spurs an early advantage with Gilberto and Darren Bent adding to the scoring. A 2-1 defeat to Manchester City came three days after the heartbreaking exit from the UEFA Cup. Next opponents Chelsea were naturally looking for revenge after the Carling Cup Final. Goals from Jonathan Woodgate, Berbatov, Tom Huddlestone and a wonderful equaliser from Robbie Keane helped record another 4-4 draw at White Hart Lane and end another memorable game against Spurs' West London rivals. A 2-1 win at home to Portsmouth secured a 'double' over the eventual FA Cup winners. Spurs' next home match against Newcastle turned out to be a game to forget as the visitors registered a 4-1 win confirming their Premier League status for the following season.

APRIL
Pld: 4 W: 0 D: 4 L: 0

April proved to be a month of frustration with four consecutive 1-1 draws. The sequence began with a credible draw at Blackburn. Dimitar Berbatov gave Spurs the lead but Morten Gamst Pedersen levelled the scoring just before half-time. A Jonathan Grounds own goal put Spurs in front against Middlesbrough, but a Stewart Downing long-range effort was enough to give 'Boro a point. Berbatov was on the score sheet again against Wigan, who were a vastly improved side under Steve Bruce. The fourth 1-1 draw saw Bolton claim a much-needed point in their battle against relegation.

May
Pld: 2 W: 1 D: 0 L: 1

A Robbie Keane goal at Reading gave Spurs a welcome win in a dominant display. A 2-0 defeat at home to Liverpool put an end to a very disappointing league campaign. Spurs reached 11th place in January and remained there until the end of 2007/08. A plethora of goals, significant landmarks and unforgettable matches were the highlight of the league season but consistency will be top of the agenda as Spurs

SPURS IN EUROPE 2007/2008

After winning the Carling Cup, Spurs soon focused upon adding the UEFA Cup to the trophy cabinet. However, a heartbreaking penalty shootout defeat to PSV Eindhoven sent the Lilywhites crashing from the tournament in the last sixteen.

UEFA CUP 1st Round 1st Leg

TOTTENHAM HOTSPUR 6
ANORTHOSIS FAMAGUSTA 1

UEFA CUP 1st Round 2nd Leg

ANORTHOSIS FAMAGUSTA 1
TOTTENHAM HOTSPUR 1
(Spurs win 7-2 on aggregate)

Goals from Younes Kaboul, Michael Dawson, Robbie Keane, Darren Bent and a double from Jermain Defoe all but secured Tottenham's place in the group stages of the UEFA Cup. With a 6-1 aggregate lead, Spurs were able to rest Dimitar Berbatov, Pascal Chimbonda, Jermaine Jenas, and Aaron Lennon. Gareth Bale and Keane were available on the bench. As a result, the game only came to life when Fabinho gave the home side the lead early in the second half. Substitutes Bale and Keane linked-up well, with the Republic of Ireland captain equalising in the 78th minute.

UEFA CUP ROUND TWO GROUP G (GAME ONE)

TOTTENHAM HOTSPUR 1
GETAFE CLUB DE FUTBOL 2

Spurs began Group G in disappointing fashion as goals from De La Red & Braulio gave Getafe all three points. This was only Spurs' second home defeat in their European history. Jermain Defoe was the Spurs goal scorer in Martin Jol's final match in charge.

UEFA CUP ROUND TWO GROUP G (GAME TWO)

HAPOEL TEL-AVIV 0
TOTTENHAM HOTSPUR 2

Spurs secured their first three points in Group G as goals from Robbie Keane and Dimitar Berbatov ensured a comfortable victory over the Israeli side

UEFA CUP ROUND TWO GROUP G (GAME THREE)

TOTTENHAM HOTSPUR 3
AALBORG BK 2

The prospects of reaching the next stages of the competition were given a huge boost in this thriller against our Danish Group G rivals. Spurs produced a superb comeback following some inspired substitutions from Juande Ramos. Trailing 2-0 at half time, Ramos introduced Darren Bent and Tom Huddlestone. Huddlestone made an immediate impact, setting Dimitar Berbatov free to bring Spurs back into the game. The equaliser came in quick succession, Berbatov this time presenting a chance to Steed Malbranque, who hammered it home. The imminence of the next goal could be felt across the Lane, and it arrived when substitute Bent fired home a close-range shot after Aalborg failed to clear a Gareth Bale free-kick.

UEFA CUP ROUND TWO GROUP G (GAME FOUR)

ANDERLECHT 1

TOTTENHAM HOTSPUR 1

Spurs guaranteed a place in the UEFA Cup Round of 32 with this draw in Belgium. Anderlecht took the lead against the run of play but a Dimitar Berbatov penalty three minutes later ensured our progress into the next stage.

UEFA CUP Round of 32 (1ST LEG)

SLAVIA PRAGUE 1

TOTTENHAM HOTSPUR 2

UEFA CUP ROUND OF 32 2ND LEG

TOTTENHAM HOTSPUR 1

SLAVIA PRAGUE 1

(Spurs win 3-2 on aggregate)

Spurs scored two priceless away goals as Dimitar Berbatov and Robbie Keane created a 2-1 lead in Prague. Spurs dominated throughout but were unable to capitalise on the chances created. The second leg was a tighter affair. With only three days remaining until the Carling Cup Final, preserving the fitness of key players was paramount. Jamie O'Hara scored his first goal for Spurs, but Slavia equalised early in the second half to create some nervous moments in the closing minutes. However, Spurs held on to claim a place in the last 16 after a 1-1 draw.

UEFA CUP LAST 16 1ST LEG

TOTTENHAM HOTSPUR 0

PSV EINDHOVEN 1

UEFA CUP LAST 16 2ND LEG

PSV EINDHOVEN 0

TOTTENHAM HOTSPUR 1 AET

(PSV Eindhoven win 6-5 on penalties)

The atmosphere at White Hart Lane was electric prior to the 1st leg. Gareth Bale and Chris Gunter paraded the Carling Cup around the ground to the sound of huge applause from the supporters. An error from Gilberto allowed Man of the Match Jefferson Farfan to strike, putting the Dutch League leaders in firm control for the decisive second leg. A stunning goal from Dimitar Berbatov in the second leg took the game into extra-time but Spurs were to endure penalty-shootout heartbreak. Pascal Chimbonda missed a crucial penalty, allowing PSV to win the game. Juande Ramos' love affair with the UEFA Cup will continue in 2008/2009 as Spurs enter the competition for the third successive season.

THE FA CUP

Tottenham Hotspur have always had a great love affair with the FA Cup. But after the heroics in thrashing Arsenal 5-1 in the Carling Cup, a trip to Old Trafford days later saw the end of the FA Cup campaign for this season at the 4th-round stage.

FA CUP ROUND THREE

TOTTENHAM HOTSPUR 2
READING 2

Seven days after the amazing 6-4 victory over Reading in the league, Steve Coppell's side returned to White Hart Lane. Reading took the lead on 25 minutes when a Paul Robinson error resulted in him taking the ball behind his own line. Spurs soon recovered from this setback when Dimitar Berbatov beat Reading keeper Adam Federici. Berbatov struck again with a penalty after Liam Rosenior fouled Robbie Keane in the area. With Spurs now leading, the momentum of the game lay firmly with the home side. A Keane goal was disallowed due to a foul by Pascal Chimbonda, but Spurs continued to seek a match winner. However, in the final quarter Stephen Hunt managed to find the back of the net for the visitors. As both sides looked for a victory, the final event of the match was in fact Tom Huddlestone's sending off. A winning goal was not realised by either team. With a final score of 2-2, the goal tally between the clubs was a massive fourteen in seven days!

FA CUP ROUND THREE REPLAY

READING 0
TOTTENHAM HOTSPUR 1

Spurs approached another match against Reading with a clear determination to finish the job. The match winner was achieved by Robbie Keane in the 15th minute as he pounced on the rebound after Younes Kaboul had headed a Jermaine Jenas corner against the crossbar. As comfortable winners, Spurs oozed superiority during this match. It was not a match worthy of the title 'thriller' as the previous two meetings had been, but was an important victory nonetheless.

FA CUP ROUND FOUR

MANCHESTER UNITED 3
TOTTENHAM HOTSPUR 1

Naturally, Manchester United were always going to be tougher opponents in the fourth round. As another club steeped in FA Cup history, they were equally keen to progress to the next round. This made for an interesting and lively match. Robbie Keane opened the scoring in the 24th minute. Spurs' early vigour was soon matched by Manchester United, culminating in a Carlos Tevez strike before half-time. Attempts on goal by Jermaine Jenas and Aaron Lennon could have given Spurs the advantage; however, in the end, Cristiano Ronaldo was the match winner with a penalty and then another goal later in the second-half. The loss ended Spurs' FA Cup run for the year, focusing attentions firmly onto the Carling Cup Final.

DAVID BENTLEY
"IT MEANS THE WORLD TO JOIN TOTTENHAM"

David Bentley became our fourth major signing of the summer after the England international joined from Blackburn Rovers. The boyhood Spurs fan made an immediate impression, scoring on his debut one day after signing for the club in the 2-0 win over Celtic in Rotterdam. His reaction to scoring his first goal for the club was one of pride – holding the Tottenham badge proudly in his hand. Bentley said: "There is a piece of my heart at this club and as soon as I knew Tottenham were interested in me, there was nowhere else I wanted to go. I was trying my hardest to come here, every day on the phone. A lot of my friends are season-ticket holders."

Bentley started his career at North London rivals Arsenal and while he was highly regarded at the club, his chances of a significant run in the first-team were hindered by the form of Robert Pires and Freddie Ljungberg during Arsenal's successful title-winning run. His lack of first-team action resulted in a loan move to Premier League new boys Norwich. His performances for Norwich saw him move to Blackburn Rovers initially on loan which turned into a permanent deal in 2006. His move to Ewood Park enabled Bentley to flourish into the player Arsene Wenger saw, when he made him train with the Arsenal first-team at only 16 years of age. Bentley scored a hat-trick for Blackburn against Manchester United – the first player ever to do so in the Premier League. He was an integral part of the club's successful 2006-07 season where Blackburn reached the UEFA Cup.

His great form for Blackburn led to a call-up to the England side. This came soon after he became the first Englishman to score at the new Wembley stadium where he scored a free-kick against Italy Under-21s. Bentley will hope to become a firm fixture in Fabio Capello's squad for the forthcoming World Cup Qualifying campaign. Primarily on Bentley's mind however is a successful career at Tottenham. After being part of the club's pre-season tour of Holland, his thoughts are on the season ahead. He added: "I want to be as successful as possible at Spurs and I'll give my all every day to do that. If I do that and everyone else does that in the dressing room, we'll be going places because the talent is here. I want to be part of something special, something that will grow and grow. A club like this deserves it."

Bentley says Paul Gascoigne was his childhood Spurs idol, looking back on an exciting period for Spurs with 'Gazza' at the forefront for club and country. Bentley himself has high hopes for his Tottenham future. "We can do anything we want, anything we put our minds to. You've seen what Juande Ramos did last year; the fitness and level of play has risen and I want to be part of that, hopefully we'll keep progressing and doing well."

JAMIE O'HARA
YOUNG PLAYER OF THE YEAR

When Jamie O'Hara started the season, it's fair to say that he would never have imagined being awarded the Tottenham Hotspur Young Player of the Year by May. Loaned out to Millwall at the start of the season, it looked as if the loan spell would be extended to the end of the season. However, Juande Ramos was extremely impressed with O'Hara's work-ethic and decided to hold him at White Hart Lane.

O'Hara made his first league appearance in the Spurs colours late last year. He made an important contribution to the 1-0 victory over Portsmouth at Fratton Park. His first appearance in the starting line-up came against fierce rivals Arsenal, a challenge to which he rose remarkably, despite the 2-1 defeat. In another fantastic performance away to Manchester City in the Carling Cup, O'Hara set-up the Steed Malbranque goal which assured Spurs a place in the Semi Final of the competition. O'Hara's first goal came against Slavia Prague in the UEFA Cup, a significant achievement for any young player.

O'Hara is an example of one of the few players to have crossed the North London divide between the Arsenal and Spurs Academy. He has been applauded by many footballing critics and is therefore considered a first-rate acquisition for the blue-and-white half of North London. Prior to his first team starts he impressed Tottenham officials at Youth and Reserve level.

At international level, O'Hara has represented the England Under-16s, 17s and 18s. His good form at Spurs over December 2007 and January 2008 resulted in a call up to the England Under-21 side against the Republic of Ireland in February. It is fair to say that if he continues to improve in the next few years, O'Hara could be considered for a full England cap.

O'Hara's love for the club is well-known and he has dreamt of playing for Spurs since childhood. He described his rise to the first team ranks saying:

"Coming from a Spurs background, it's been great to play at White Hart Lane. I'd waited a number of years to put on the shirt and make my debut, and it's been a dream since then."

The new season will see the spotlight pointed at O'Hara having gained the Young Player of the Year accolade. His obvious love for the club combined with his promising skill and ability mean the future is certainly bright for the popular midfielder.

JUANDE RAMOS

HEAD COACH

Juande Ramos made an immediate impact at White Hart Lane. With expectations high for the 2008/2009 campaign, who could fill Spurs fans with more hope than a man of such unquestionable talent?

Ramos' two-year managerial reign in Seville was hugely successful. He delivered consistent results and collected five trophies including two UEFA Cup successes. He is a popular figure who is revered across Europe for his obvious talents. With such a record, it was only a matter of time before the Premier League came calling for his services.

Ramos joined the club in October 2007 and his introduction had a marked effect upon the team. Soon, Spurs had climbed

GUS POYET

FIRST TEAM COACH

Gustavo Augusto Poyet Domínguez was born November 15, 1967 in Montevideo, Uruguay. He played for French side Grenoble and Argentine giants River Plate before moving to Real Zaragoza. Here, he made 239 appearances scoring 63 goals. Gus captained the European Cup Winners Cup winning side which beat Arsenal 2-1 in 1994 after Nayim scored that famous goal in extra-time. Poyet's next move was to England in 1997 joining Chelsea on a free transfer. He got his hands on the European Cup Winners Cup again in his first year at the club after victory over VFB Stuttgart which was the beginning of four successful years at Stamford Bridge. He scored 49 goals in 145 appearances. Poyet signed for Spurs in 2001 to join-up with Teddy Sheringham who had returned to the club from Manchester United. It didn't take long for Poyet to endear himself to the White Hart Lane crowd. One of his Spurs highlights was scoring a last-minute equaliser in a North London derby. A leader on the field, it was not surprising to see Gus take an early interest in coaching after leaving Spurs. He joined Swindon Town as a player/assistant manager to Dennis Wise but his stay at the club was short-lived. Leeds approached both Wise and Poyet after impressive starts at the County Ground, giving them the opportunity to try to turn around the fortunes of the Yorkshire side. Poyet became a very popular figure with the Leeds supporters and many even asked him to re-register as a player after scoring a fantastic volley in a pre-season game for the club. His work at Leeds was recognised by Spurs and he was appointed first-team coach under Juande Ramos in October 2007. His appointment was a welcome one and his approachable demeanour and good sense of humour is never lost on the media. Poyet always offers interesting and enjoyable post-match interviews. The impact of Juande Ramos has been often talked about and rightly so, but no manager can succeed without a strong backroom team. Any success Spurs achieve in season 2008/2009 will have had a major influence from both Ramos and Poyet.

the Premier League table and were notably progressing in two cup competitions, the UEFA and Carling Cup. This was certainly a flying start for Ramos.

By February 2008, Ramos had become a Spurs hero. His leadership had helped secure victory in the Carling Cup and the return of silverware to White Hart Lane – just where it should be. This win was made all the more glorious by the skilled disposal of London rivals Arsenal and Chelsea.

Ramos' own playing career was cut short at the age of 28 after suffering a knee injury. By 1992, he was entering the field of management and has since taken charge of a wide range of clubs. During his career, he has had spells at C.D.Alcoyano, Levante UD, C.D.Logroñés, F.C.Barcelona B, U.E.Lleida, Rayo Vallecano, Real Betis Balompié, R.C.D.Espanyol de Barcelona, Málaga C.F., Sevilla F.C. and now Spurs.

Ramos has shown a desire for fast paced, attacking football from all the clubs he has managed throughout his career. His Sevilla squad combined a strong defensive record with a unique style of attack. At times, Sevilla played some of the best football in Europe, resulting in a Champions League finish in La Liga and the team acquiring numerous trophies.

Ramos pays particular attention to the fitness and diet of footballers under his charge. On joining Spurs, he introduced a new exercise and dietary regime in order to begin the process of making the team his own. On page 34 you will find a number of dietary hints and tips if you are eager to be as healthy as Ramos' blue-and-white army.

Whilst Spurs fans across London, the UK and the world have all fallen in love with Ramos, the admiration is mutual:

> "I was hugely impressed with the Spurs fans both home and away when Sevilla played Spurs [in the UEFA CUP, 2006/2007]".

So, under the watchful eye of Juande, there are plenty of highs to look forward to in the coming months. With a winning combination of tactical prowess and the strict fitness regime, who knows what dizzying heights Ramos' men may achieve this season.

CARLING
MANSION

CARLING CUP FINAL

24 FEB 2008 / WEMBLEY

PLAYER PROFILES

HEURELHO GOMES

Gomes joined us from Dutch champions PSV Eindhoven in July, 2008. The Brazilian international was an ever-present member of PSV's title-winning squad in 2007-08, when he conceded only 24 goals in 34 league games. He made his name at Cruzeiro in Brazil, debuting in 2002 before securing his move to PSV in 2004. Gomes is likely to become a crowd favourite as the season progresses

CESAR SANCHEZ

The Spaniard joined Zaragoza in 2005, having previously spent five years at Real Madrid where he earned a Champions League winners medal in 2002 after starting the final against Bayer Leverkusen. Cesar, 36, began his playing career with Real Valladolid, earning an international cap for his country against Germany in August, 2000. He will bring a wealth of experience to our goalkeeping ranks and provide very able back-up to Heurelho Gomes in the Tottenham goal.

BEN ALNWICK

Ben joined Spurs from Sunderland in 2007 with Marton Fulop heading in the opposite direction to the Stadium of Light. After loan spells at Luton & Leicester Ben will be looking to establish himself among the first team picture at White Hart Lane in the coming season.

OSCAR JANSSON

Oscar has regularly represented Sweden at youth level. He began his career at Karlsund HFK before moving to Spurs in 2007. He joined Juande Ramos and the first-team on their pre-season trip to Spain. Oscar also played in our 5-1 pre-season victory over Leyton Orient.

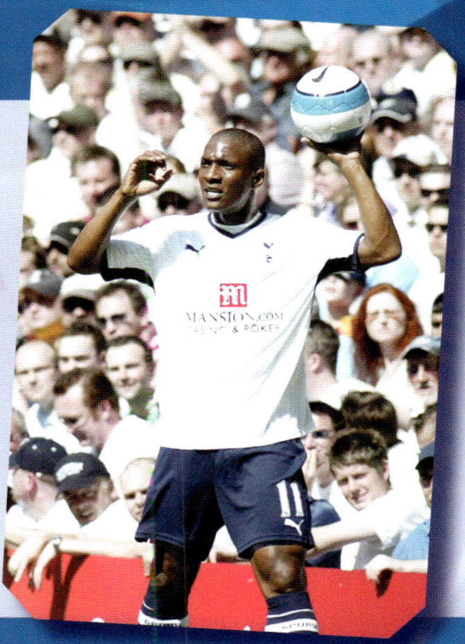

GILBERTO

32 year old Brazilian international left back, signed in January 2008 from Hertha Berlin. Gilberto scored in the 4-0 victory over West Ham, coming off the bench to contribute to a memorable day. A strong ball winner with pace, Gilberto looks likely to play a key role this season.

GARETH BALE

Gareth signed from Southampton in 2007 and made an instant impact. In 12 games for Spurs, he played at left back and left-wing scoring three goals including a free-kick against Arsenal. Sadly, his season ended in December due to a serious ankle injury, but Bale will be 'one to watch' in the new season

PLAYER PROFILES

MICHAEL DAWSON

The popular defender was unlucky to miss out on a chance in the Carling Cup Final after sustaining an injury against Derby County. He scored two goals last season. Will hope to add a full England cup to his collection of Youth and Under-21 honours.

LEDLEY KING

The Spurs captain only featured 10 times last season due to his continuing injury problems. His appearance at the Carling Cup Final was characteristically outstanding and Ledley could be described as an immaculate defender. Hopes are high for an increased presence of the popular skipper this season.

JONATHAN WOODGATE

Already a White Hart Lane hero after scoring the winning goal in the Carling Cup Final, the England international was a very welcome addition to the side after signing for the club in January. Hoping to put his injury problems to one side, Woodgate is one of the finest defenders in English football.

ALAN HUTTON

Another signing to make an immediate impression, Alan signed from Rangers in early 2008. He won a Carling Cup winner's medal in only his third game for Spurs but was unable to be eligible for the UEFA Cup games. The Scottish international appeared in the side which beat France 1-0 in a Euro 2008 qualifier.

CHRIS GUNTER

18 year old Welsh international full-back signed from Cardiff in the January transfer window. He made his debut in the FA Cup win at Reading. Chris can play at left or right-back and has recently played at centre-back for Wales.

BENOIT ASSOU-EKOTTO

It's fair to say Spurs supporters have yet to see the best of Benoit. Signed from RC Lens in 2006, Assou-Ekotto has suffered from a succession of knee injuries since joining from the French side. Benoit will hope to stay injury-free in the coming season to help kick-start his Tottenham career after some impressive performances in pre-season

PLAYER PROFILES

DIDIER ZOKORA

Didier has shown his versatility in the past year looking more than comfortable in a central defensive role. Always reliable when called upon, Didier continues to represent the Ivory Coast as he reaches his third season at Spurs.

JERMAINE JENAS

A memorable season for the central midfielder. Jermaine scored at home and away against Arsenal in Spurs' Carling Cup Semi-Final victory. Jenas also scored the first goal under new England Manager Fabio Capello. Jermaine captained the Spurs side that won the pre-season Feyenoord Tournament in Holland.

ADEL TAARABT

Taarabt will go into the new season hoping to play more first-team games. He is certainly a talented midfielder and has impressed at Reserve level.

TOM HUDDLESTONE

A superb passer of the ball who is also able to cover at centre-back, but has primarily played from the midfield this season, including his England under-21 appearances. Tom was selected by Fabio Capello for his 30-man England squad for the two end of season friendlies.

JAMIE O'HARA

Last season was Jamie's debut in the Premier League, and it proved to be a great success. Jamie was named Young Player of the Season after his efforts in league and cup matches.

LUKA MODRIC

The Croatian international midfielder joins after playing a starring role for Croatia in the 2008 European Championships. The 22-year-old played a key role in his country's run to the quarter-finals and was widely regarded as one of the players of the tournament.

PLAYER PROFILES

AARON LENNON

Aaron's speed on the wing is well known and feared in the Premier League. Young Player of the Season two seasons ago, he has continued to impress. Aaron was selected by Sven Goran Eriksson to play in the 2006 World Cup and is likely to continue to gain international caps.

DAVID BENTLEY

David joined from Blackburn Rovers in July 2008. The England international made 133 appearances for the Ewood Park side - scoring 21 goals - after initially joining on loan from Arsenal in August 2005, the move being made permanent in January 2006. The 23-year-old has now won six senior England caps after previously representing his country at B, Under-21 and Under-20 level. Bentley was the first player to score at the new Wembley Stadium after his free-kick against Italy Under-21's

GIOVANI DOS SANTOS

Highly-rated forward completed his move to the Lane from Barcelona in June, 2008. A star of the FIFA U17 World Championships in 2005 and FIFA U20 World Championships in 2007, Giovani, still just 19, already has full international honours with Mexico. Giovani made 28 senior appearances for Barcelona in 2007-08, scoring three goals, after displaying his credentials in the B team, where he made 27 appearances and netted five times

DARREN BENT

Darren was the club's record signing at £16.5 million in 2007, scoring eight goals in 15 starts in his first season. Scored in our 4-0 victory over West Ham and was on hand to score the winning goal in our 3-2 win over Aalborg in the UEFA Cup. Bent scored four goals as Spurs beat Norwich 5-1 in our pre-season friendly at Carrow Road in July then netted a hat-trick two days later against Leyton Orient.

CHELSEA

- 2 TOTTENHAM

FITNESS AND NUTRITION

Juande Ramos is known to endorse the importance of fitness and nutrition, along with Spurs first team coach Marcos Alvarez. Here are some hints and tips to help follow a healthy diet:

- Most importantly, following a balanced diet will leave you fit, healthy and full of energy. A combination of carbohydrates, proteins and vegetables for vitamins is the key to success.
- Chicken is high in protein, essential for developing muscle strength. It is also low in fat, making it a healthier option than red meat.
- Brown rice is a fantastic, and healthy, source of energy. The body breaks this carbohydrate down slowly, meaning it fills you up for longer and provides consistent energy levels.
- Similar to brown rice, wholemeal pasta provides a steady level of energy for the body to use.
- Everybody likes a sugary treat. However, it is important to regulate how much sugar you eat for a number of reasons. For example, sugar is detrimental to dental health and also affects blood-sugar levels leaving you feeling lethargic after an initial boost.
- Drinking approximately 2 litres of water a day is beneficial to your well-being. It will energise you, reduce tiredness and prepare you for the rigours of exercise.

- An important part of your complete well-being is Vitamin C, which can help guard against infections and colds. Vitamin C is most obviously found in citrus fruits such as oranges. Or, you could try something new and drink a glass of cranberry juice.

- Fish is an important super-food. Not only is it another source of vital protein but oily fish is high in Omega-3s which are reputed to improve brain power and concentration whilst playing an important football match.

- Bananas have a wealth of uses. They are a cheap source of energy and are effective before and after exercise. Make your own healthy smoothies by blending a banana with other tasty fruits such as strawberries, apples or pears. A great way to stave off a hunger for sugar.

- Iron is essential in a healthy diet. It prevents tiredness, lethargy and most seriously, anaemia. Iron is found in a wide range of foods from red meat, to spinach, to apricots.

'Information supplied by Sam Erith, Tottenham Hotspur's Head of Sports Science.'

1

2

3

4

WHO ARE YOU

ANSWERS PG. 58

W	A	D	D	L	E	G	P	H	J	E	E	C	B	B
X	R	F	H	D	Y	P	R	C	D	O	S	M	L	V
B	D	C	G	D	T	M	S	E	N	S	E	V	A	C
N	I	V	F	I	S	B	A	W	A	Q	Q	Y	N	M
I	L	K	V	D	N	Q	X	B	Z	V	M	N	C	G
C	E	L	G	C	E	O	S	L	B	T	E	N	H	M
H	S	I	L	X	G	H	L	U	Y	U	L	S	F	L
O	G	N	A	V	C	A	T	A	X	L	T	L	L	I
L	F	S	M	Q	A	H	O	D	D	L	E	T	O	N
S	Y	M	C	M	A	C	K	A	Y	C	S	N	W	E
O	G	A	C	G	H	J	K	Z	K	G	A	B	E	K
N	D	N	M	Q	E	U	M	B	O	B	A	Q	R	E
H	U	N	P	E	R	R	Y	M	A	N	P	H	L	R
L	P	A	Q	L	I	L	Y	D	Z	M	N	U	I	I
V	C	W	B	J	E	N	N	I	N	G	S	A	L	Y

Can you find the names of FOURTEEN Spurs legends in this word search? Words can go horizontally, vertically and diagonally

WORD SEARCH

ANSWERS PG. 59

Luka Modric became our first senior summer signing of the season when the deal was announced in April. The highly-rated midfielder was coveted by many of Europe's top clubs but his decision to join Spurs gave the club a big boost for the season ahead.

Modric played in the Bosnian league as a teenager. In 2003 he was named Bosnian League Player of the Year. He next progressed into the Croatian league after joining Inter Zapresic and later Dinamo Zagreb in 2005. Within a year he had become part of the increasingly impressive Croatian national team. Modric has achieved a number of caps for his country including the decisive victories over England in the Euro 2008 qualifiers. Having signed for Spurs, Modric was present at the 1-1 draw with Bolton Wanderers. With the season still in progress, the acquisition of Modric was a clear statement that Spurs were going to mean business in this summer's transfer market, and in the coming season.

Modric was delighted about his move to North London: "I am very lucky and proud to be here in London at Tottenham. I am also happy that the coach Juande Ramos wanted me, it is the most important thing that the coach wants you as a player. I want to show that I have the quality for Tottenham and the English Premier League and help the club achieve big results."

Modric has also made his aspirations for himself and Spurs clear, along with his high regard for the English league: "I want to play for Tottenham in international football - Champions League or UEFA Cup games. I want to achieve big things with the club and be in the top group of teams in the Premier League. The speed of the game is appealing and great stadiums with many fans. The speed and tempo of the games is a big factor."

Modric will certainly make an impact upon the Premier League. He has an innate technical skill and a remarkable ability to read the state of play in competitive football matches. He is also ready and determined to tackle the physical nature of the Premier League. Modric once stated "someone who can play in the Bosnian league can play anywhere", due to the physical nature of this league. His performances at the European Championships have been applauded by all quarters of the footballing world and despite heading home after a heart-breaking quarter-final defeat by Turkey, his impact in Austria and Switzerland will not be forgotten.

It is widely agreed that Modric is one of the most promising talents in European football. Slaven Bilic, his national coach, rates him as one of the world's best midfielders and at such a young age, he is certainly a fantastic possession for any club hoping to attain high-level Premier League positions – exactly where Spurs are aiming. The coming months will be an interesting time as Modric proves whether or not he can emulate the legend-status previously filled by White Hart Lane darlings such as Glenn Hoddle, Paul Gascoigne and David Ginola.

"It is a dream for me to come to a big club like Spurs."

Another important and, yet again exciting, signing at White Hart Lane came in early June. Giovani dos Santos, hotly tipped as another potential footballing megastar adds a further level of promise to the 2008/2009 squad.

Signed from Barcelona, the Mexican international is another shining example of the way Spurs can attract key players due to the prospects these youngsters perceive to be possible at the Lane:

"It is a dream for me to come to a big club like Spurs. I've come here to further explore my qualities and give my all for my new team. As a young player I have come to a club where I feel there are many opportunities for me."

Juande Ramos described his pleasure on signing dos Santos:

"This is a young player with a lot of potential, whom I have watched for some time and I am delighted he has joined the squad"

Dos Santos' versatility and overt strength have been recognised by club officials. Ramos commented on the way the Mexican "operates well in different positions and, above all, is technically excellent". Tottenham's Director of Football Damien Comolli also admires dos Santos' "physical power and explosivity", which will be highly complementary to the role of Luka Modric.

Dos Santos will undoubtedly be another player in sharp focus for all fans, and if his potential is fulfilled, the products of his skills will be fantastic to watch.

BECOME A ONE HOTSPUR JUNIOR MEMBER AND GET TICKET PRIORITY AT THE LANE

TOTTENHAM HOTSPUR

OTHER BENEFITS INCLUDE

- The opportunity to buy a guest ticket for home league matches during a priority period and subject to availability
- Priority period over non-One Hotspur members to purchase away/cup match tickets
- A special One Hotspur Folder packed with the following goodies:
  - A unique One Hotspur Sweatband with built in watch
  - A pencil case with stationery and One Hotspur Notebook
  - A One Hotspur Gym bag
  - A special One Hotspur torch pen that projects the Club badge onto a wall or ceiling
- Christmas and Birthday cards
- Plus much more

ONE HOTSPUR JUNIOR
THE OFFICIAL MEMBERSHIP

JOIN TODAY, CALL 0844 844 0102 OR VISIT TOTTENHAMHOTSPUR.COM

GARETH BALE

DANNY ROSE

TROY ARCHIBALD-HENVILLE

Danny joined us from Leeds United at the start of the 2007-08 season and has largely featured for the Reserve side under Clive Allen. After some impressive performances Rose was an unused sub for the first team against Sunderland. He is a skilful attacking midfielder who reads the game well, also possessing a good tackling and passing ability. A shin injury restricted his number of appearances for the reserves and potentially hampered further substitute appearances for the first team. However, the very fact he was named in Ramos' squad in his first year at the club speaks volumes for a player who has featured regularly at England Youth level.

Captain of the Tottenham Reserves, Troy had a very successful 2007/08 season. Injury problems had previously restricted his development but he has since made significant strides forward resulting in his captaincy. His good form for the Reserves saw him onto the bench for Spurs' away match at Arsenal and home match against Wigan Athletic. Troy is equally adaptable at right-back but has clearly impressed as a centre-back and it is likely this will be his preferred position as his development continues.

TOMAS PEKHART

JOHN BOSTOCK

Tomas has represented the Czech Republic at Under-16, Under-17, Under-18, Under-20 and Under-21 levels. He played in the Final of the UEFA Under-17 Championships in Luxembourg for his country, and scored seven times in 18 appearances at that level in 2005-06. He has scored five goals in five matches for the under-21 side. Joined Spurs in 2006 from Slavia Prague and has scored a number of goals at reserve level. A strong first season for Pekhart in 2006-07 resulted in 19 goals in 20 matches for the Spurs Academy.

A player with massive potential, John joined the club from Crystal Palace this summer. While a number of top sides declared their interest in the England Youth international, Bostock made it clear that White Hart Lane was his preferred destination. Speaking after signing, John added: "I am definitely ready to make this move and Spurs is the team I wanted to join. I feel this is a club with a great future and this is where I want to be to develop my potential and improve as a player." The 16-year-old midfielder was previously a schoolboy with Crystal Palace, making his first team debut as a second-half substitute against Watford in October 2007. He went on to make a further two starts as well as two appearances as a substitute for the Championship club. He will continue his development in the reserve team for 2008/09 but after bursting onto the scene at Selhurst Park at such a young age we're bound to see him in a Spurs shirt at a packed White Hart Lane sooner rather than later.

125 YEARS SUPER QUIZ

On October 1st 2007, Super Spurs celebrated their 125th Anniversary. It's a grand old team to play for and it's a grand old team to see, so if you know your history, try this Super Size Spurs Quiz.

1. Who scored an own goal for Spurs in a 2-1 victory in the 1991 FA Cup Final?
2. True or false? Spurs once played in red shirts.
3. Who did we beat in the European Cup Winners Cup Final in 1963?
4. Who scored the winning goal for Spurs in the 1999 League Cup Final?
5. Who did we play in Juande Ramos' first match for the club?
6. What do Damien Comolli and Didier Zokora have in common?

7. Spurs have had three different home grounds. Where did we play before White Hart Lane?

8. Who wore the Number 5 shirt in the FA Cup Final Replay against Manchester City in 1981?

9. George Graham managed both Spurs and Arsenal. Which other manager has crossed the North London divide?

10. How many times have Spurs won the Football League Cup?

11. Which former Spurs player once cost the club £99,999?

12. True or false? World Cup winning Manager Sir Alf Ramsey once played for Spurs.

13. Which former German international signed for Spurs in 1994?

14. "I would run through brick walls for Spurs". Who made this famous quotation?

15. True or false? Spurs used to ground-share with West Ham.

16. Who did Spurs beat in the 1961 FA Cup Final?

17. Who did Spurs face in the 1961 FA Charity Shield (Now named the Community Shield)?

18. Which former Spurs Manager introduced the famous 'push and run' style of football?

19. What nationality was former captain Danny Blanchflower?

20. True or false? Gilberto is the first Brazilian player to play for Spurs in the first team.

Heurelho Gomes became our third major summer signing in June after his transfer from PSV Eindhoven. Gomes was an integral part of the PSV side that knocked Spurs out of the UEFA Cup, saving a Jermaine Jenas penalty. However, the Brazilian international will now be a key part of our domestic and European campaign.

Gomes started his career at Brazilian side Cruzeiro and after two successful years in his home nation he was transferred to PSV in July 2004. His four years in Holland have resulted in four consecutive league titles, the Dutch Cup in 2005 and also a Semi-Final finish in the Champions League in his first season.

Gomes quickly became a crowd favourite in Holland, keeping a clean sheet for 971 consecutive minutes in his first season in Eindhoven. His throwing ability has become a trademark. He is able to throw the ball deep into the opposition area which has led to PSV scoring on numerous occasions on the counter attack. Showing his emotions also helped him win the hearts of the PSV supporters. However, his celebrations have led to injury. In a match with Feyenoord Gomes celebrated with Phillip Cocu, only to injure himself in the process but he stayed on the field in a crucial 1-0 victory.

"The reception I have received at Spurs has been fantastic and I hope we can have a good season."

While Gomes looks back fondly on his time in Holland, he is now eagerly anticipating an exciting career ahead in England. He says: "There were some great times at Eindhoven and now I hope the coming season will be equally as great in terms of success. I'm very happy to be here, all players want to play in the Premier League that is like a dream and I'm going to do my best for Tottenham.

"The English competition is a great competition- the greatest in Europe and possibly the world. There are some quality sides that we will be competing against, so it will be very difficult but I hope to achieve big things. It is all new to me at the moment- the team, the competition- but I want to do a good job and I will try my best."

Gomes returned to Holland in pre-season as Spurs won the Feyenoord Centenary Tournament, after comfortably beating Celtic and Borussia Dortmund. Gomes kept a clean sheet in both matches and overall pre-season was a great success in terms of results, fitness and team-bonding. His determination and enthusiasm in goal was clear to see in pre-season and it's very likely that Gomes will make a great impression at White Hart Lane for seasons to come.

MARCOS ALVAREZ
FIRST TEAM COACH

Marcos Álvarez arrived at Tottenham with Juande Ramos from Sevilla, where he held a similar position working primarily on the squad's fitness. Born on 24 April 1971 in Las Palmas de Gran Canaria, Alvarez played an important role in Sevilla's recent success and has played a big part in Tottenham's upturn in fortunes notably our Carling Cup win.

Ramos saw his friend joining him at White Hart Lane as crucial to his chances of success. His working relationship with Alvarez has been going strong for more than four years, since Ramos employed Alvarez when he was in charge of Malaga.

"We have our good times and bad times. It's like we are married," Alvarez said. "We have spent a lot of time together and will continue to do so for better or for worse.

"Juande made a big decision to turn down Real Betis a few years ago because they said they didn't want me. He told me that if a club didn't agree to take me then he would always turn it down. I have said the same to him that I will never work for a club that he is not at."

"To coach in the Premier League is a dream for me and Spurs are one of the best teams in the country."

The improved fitness of the Sevilla players was highlighted as a major factor in the club's ability to challenge Real Madrid and Barcelona against the odds for the La Liga title and winning five trophies in the past two seasons win including two UEFA Cups.

While Alvarez has been commended on his coaching the 37-year-old has also been credited for helping one of Spain's top bullfighters become one of the biggest celebrities in the sport.

Alvarez also pays a great deal of attention to the diet of a modern day footballer. (Turn to our nutrition page for further information).

Marcos says: "To eat healthy means there is no fried food, fatty food, no sauce on the dishes. Spanish people can eat the same kind of food, too, but if you a sportsman you have to take care of yourself better. Now there are salads and fruit, while fish and meat is grilled rather than fried."

Renowned as a real taskmaster on the training pitch, Alvarez was central to Spurs' pre-season preparations putting the players through their paces in the sweltering sun in Spain ahead of their first Premier League game of the season at Middlesbrough. The training camp in Spain proved to be a great success with the players feeling fitter than ever before as we embark on our 17th season in the Premier League.

MANSION.com
GILBERTO

ALAN HUTTON
.COM
& POKER
SPURS

DID YOU KNOW...

Here is a selection of facts and figures from the proud history of Tottenham Hotspur.

In 1890 Spurs wore red shirts!

Spurs were formed in 1882 because the cricket season had finished!

First British club to win a major European competition, winning the European Cup Winners Cup against Athletico Madrid in 1963.

Our first match with Arsenal – then Royal Arsenal– was in 1887 and was abandoned 15 minutes from time 'owing to darkness' with Spurs leading 2-1.

Spurs were the first club to win the League Cup twice after defeating Norwich in the 1973 Final.

Following the formation of the Football League in 1888, Spurs became the first and only non-league team to lift the FA Cup.

Spurs were the first football club to float shares on the London Stock Exchange in 1983.

Spurs were crowned Football League Champions and winners of the FA Cup in 1961. The first club to complete the 'Double' in the 20th century.

In October 2004, England started with three Spurs players (Jermain Defoe, Ledley King, Paul Robinson) for the first time since 1987.

First English club to have played in three major European finals after our UEFA Cup match in 1974.

Tottenham were the first club to lift the FA Cup with ribbons attached. Since 1901, the practise has been followed by every winning club since.

John Piercy became the 500th player to be used by Spurs after coming on as a substitute against Derby County on October 16th 1999.

Aaron Lennon became the youngest Spurs player ever to play in the World Cup Finals after coming on as a substitute in England's match with Trinidad & Tobago. Aaron was 19 years and 60 days old.

TO WEAR IS TO DO

The Official Tottenham Hotspur Home, Away & Third Kits for the 2008/09 Season

HOME

AWAY

THIRD

Order your Spurs kit now on line at TottenhamHotspur.com or call Mail Order 0844 499 5000.

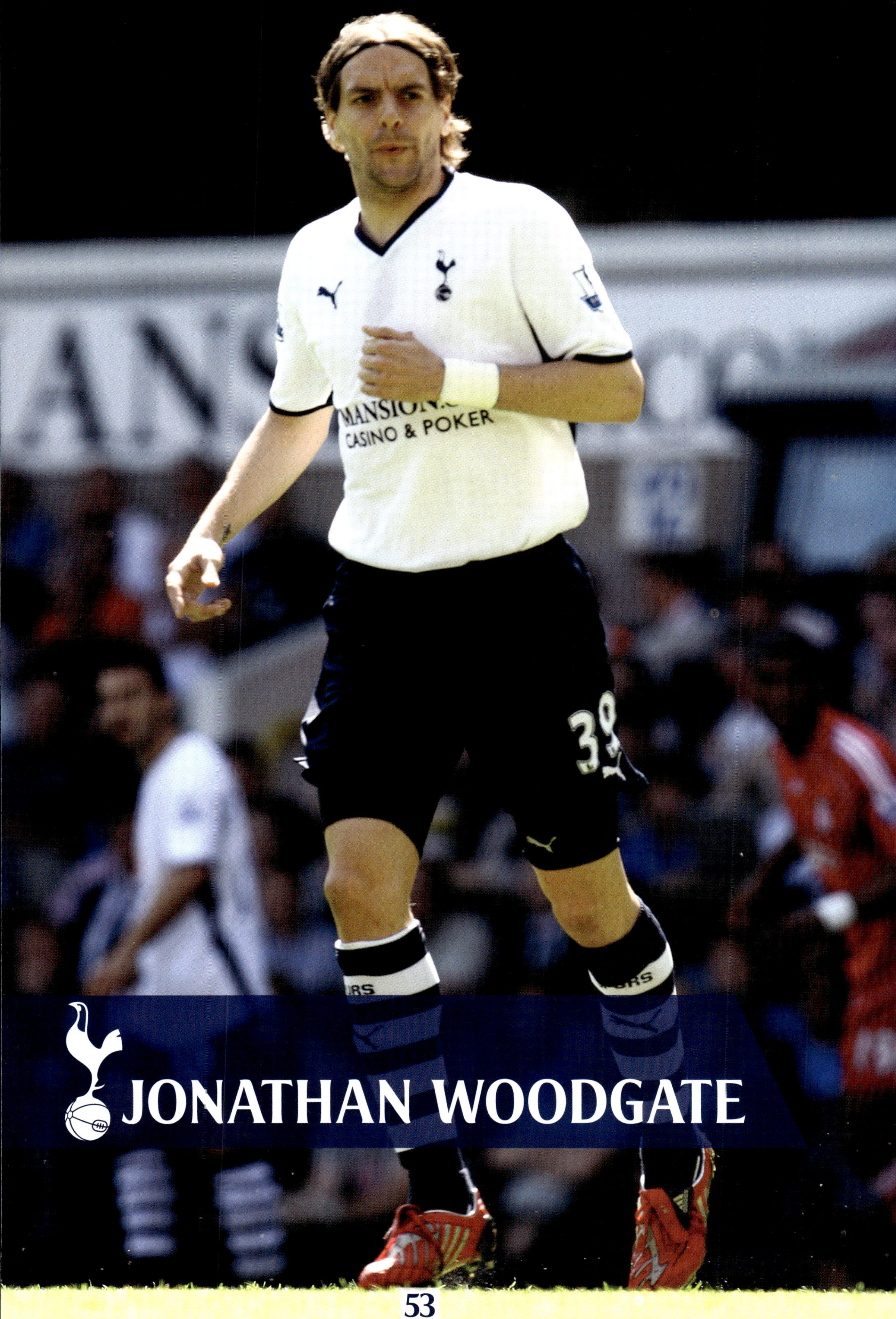
MANSION
CASINO & POKER
JONATHAN WOODGATE

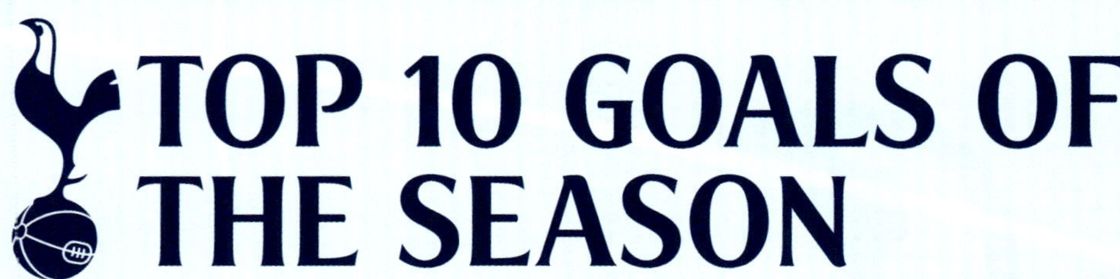

TOP 10 GOALS OF THE SEASON

The official Spurs website once again asked supporters to vote online for their favourite goal of the season. We scored 102 goals in season 2007/2008 - here is a list of the 10 most popular strikes from that campaign.

Dimitar Berbatov v Fulham, Barclays Premier League, Craven Cottage, September 1: Robbie Keane cushioned a pass over the top of Dejan Stefanovic for Berbatov to run on to, Berbatov nodded the ball down in front of him and having outpaced Stefanovic, hammered it past Antti Niemi.

Gareth Bale v Middlesbrough, Carling Cup, White Hart Lane, September 26: Robbie Keane turned George Boateng inside-out down the left as we broke from a corner, spotted Bale's run from deep and played an inch-perfect pass into his run, Bale took the ball on at full pace into the box, skipped around Brad Jones and slotted from a tight angle.

Aaron Lennon v Wigan, Barclays Premier League, White Hart Lane, November 11: Dimitar Berbatov knocked a ball square to Lennon who hit a full volley from 25 yards across Chris Kirkland into the far corner.

Steed Malbranque v Manchester City, Carling Cup, Eastlands, December 18: Dimitar Berbatov controlled the ball as we broke from a City attack and found Jamie O'Hara on the left touchline, he spotted Malbranque's run between defenders and found him with a crossfield pass that Malbranque controlled and coolly slotted past Joe Hart. Steed joined Sunderland in July. We wish him all the best for the future.

Tom Huddlestone v Fulham (2nd goal), Barclays Premier League, White Hart Lane, December 26: Aaron Lennon in possession on the right, passed the ball square to Huddlestone who flicked it up with his left foot before drilling a low volley into the far corner from 25 yards.

Dimitar Berbatov v Reading (4th goal), Barclays Premier League, White Hart Lane, December 29: Younes Kaboul hit a long pass forward, Berbatov had the strength to hold off Ivar Ingimarsson before drilling high past Marcus Hahnemann into the top corner.

Jermaine Jenas v Arsenal, Carling Cup semi-final, 2nd leg, White Hart Lane, January 22: Dimitar Berbatov cushioned a pass into Jenas, 40 yards from goal. He drove past four Arsenal players at a left-to-right angle to the edge of the box where he then hit the ball back across Lucasz Fabianski and in off the far post.

Jonathan Woodgate v Chelsea, Carling Cup Final, Wembley, February 24: Jermaine Jenas flighted in an inswinging free-kick from the left, Woodgate beat Petr Cech to it in the air and his header cannoned back off the keeper onto Woodgate again before bouncing home.

Dimitar Berbatov v PSV, UEFA Cup R16 2nd leg, Philips Stadion, March 12: Pascal Chimbonda picked out Berbatov with a pass from the right and the striker hit a superb volley without breaking stride that arrowed past keeper Gomes into the corner.

AND THE WINNER IS...

Robbie Keane v Chelsea, Barclays Premier League, White Hart Lane, March 19: The striker's superb curler into the top corner to make it 4-4 in an amazing game at the Lane in March polled 54 per cent of over 1,000 votes cast by fans on the website.

NATIONAL PRIDE

You may not realise how many current Spurs players have achieved caps for their national teams. Here is a rundown of Spurs' international roll-call.

Heurelho Gomes - Brazil

Didier Zokora – Ivory Coast

Jermaine Jenas – England

Gilberto – Brazil

Gareth Bale – Wales

Tom Huddlestone – England Under-21s

Jamie O' Hara - England Under-21s

Aaron Lennon – England

Michael Dawson – England Under-21s

Darren Bent – England

Ledley King – England

David Bentley - England

Alan Hutton – Scotland

Giovani dos Santos - Mexico

Jonathan Woodgate – England

Chris Gunter – Wales

Tomáš Pekhart – Czech Republic Under-21s

Luka Modric – Croatia

Ben Alnwick – England Under-21s

Cesar Sanchez - Spain

MANSION.COM
CASINO & POKER
22
TOM HUDDLESTONE

QUIZ ANSWERS...

125 YEARS SUPER QUIZ PG.44-45

1. Des Walker
2. True
3. Athletico Madrid
4. Allan Nielsen
5. Blackpool
6. They both joined Spurs from French club Saint-Étienne
7. Northumberland Park
8. Ricardo 'Ricky' Villa
9. Terry Neill
10. Four
11. Jimmy Greaves
12. True
13. Jurgen Klinsmann
14. Graham Roberts
15. False
16. Leicester City
17. England Select XI
18. Arthur Rowe
19. Northern Ireland
20. True

WHO ARE YOU PG.36

1

Jonathan Woodgate

2

Didier Zokora

3

Ledley King

4

Jermaine Jenas

WORD SEARCH PG.37

W	A	D	D	L	E	G	P	H	J	E	E	C	B	B
X	R	F	H	D	Y	P	R	C	D	O	S	M	L	V
B	D	C	G	D	T	M	S	E	N	S	E	V	A	C
N	I	V	F	I	S	B	A	W	A	Q	Q	Y	N	M
I	L	K	V	D	N	Q	X	B	Z	V	M	N	C	G
C	E	L	G	C	E	O	S	L	B	T	E	N	H	M
H	S	I	L	X	G	H	L	U	Y	U	L	S	F	L
O	G	N	A	V	C	A	T	A	X	L	T	L	L	I
L	F	S	M	Q	A	H	O	D	D	L	E	T	O	N
S	Y	M	C	M	A	C	K	A	Y	C	S	N	W	E
O	G	A	C	G	H	J	K	Z	K	G	A	B	E	K
N	D	N	M	Q	E	U	M	B	O	B	A	Q	R	E
H	U	N	P	E	R	R	Y	M	A	N	P	H	L	R
L	P	A	Q	L	I	L	Y	D	Z	M	N	U	I	I
V	C	W	B	J	E	N	N	I	N	G	S	A	L	Y

Waddle
Hoddle
Klinsmann
Perryman
Ginola
Tull
Nicholson
Blanchflower
Ardiles
Jennings
Lineker
Greaves
Mackay
Mabbutt

RESULTS TROPHIES AND STATS

MAJOR HONOURS

Football League Champions 1950-51, 1960-61
F.A.Cup Winners 1900-01, 1920-21, 1960-61, 1961-62, 1966-67, 1980-81, 1981-82, 1990-91
Football League Cup Winners 1970-71, 1972-73, 1998-99, 2007-08
European Cup-Winners Cup Winners 1962-63
UEFA Cup Winners 1971-72, 1983-84
F.A.Charity Shield Winners .... 1920-21, 1951-52, 1961-62, 1962-63, 1967-68 (joint), 1981-82 (joint), 1991-92 (joint).
Football League Division Two Champions......... 1919-20, 1949-50

PLAYER APPEARANCES 2007/08

B Alnwick	0 (0) 0	0 (0) 0	0 (0) 0	0 (0) 0
T Archibald-Henville	0 (0) 0	0 (0) 0	0 (0) 0	0 (0) 0
B Assou-Ekotto	1 (0) 0	0 (0) 0	0 (0) 0	1 (0) 0
G Bale	8 (0) 2	0 (0) 0	1 (0) 1	1 (2) 0
D Bent	11 (16) 6	0 (0) 0	0 (1) 0	4 (4) 2
D Berbatov	33 (3) 15	2 (0) 2	6 (0) 1	7 (1) 5
K Boateng	7 (6) 0	1 (1) 0	1 (2) 0	1 (2) 0
R Cerny	13 (0) 0	2 (0) 0	2 (0) 0	3 (0) 0
P Chimbonda	31 (1) 2	2 (0) 0	6 (0) 1	9 (0) 0
M Dawson	26 (1) 1	3 (0) 0	4 (0) 0	5 (1) 1
J Defoe	3 (16) 4	1 (1) 0	2 (3) 1	2 (3) 3
A Gardner	4 (0) 1	0 (0) 0	0 (0) 0	2 (0) 0
Gilberto	3 (3) 1	0 (0) 0	0 (0) 0	1 (0) 0
C Gunter	1 (1) 0	1 (1) 0	0 (0) 0	0 (0) 0
T Huddlestone	18 (10) 3	1 (1) 0	1 (3) 1	7 (2) 0
A Hutton	14 (0) 0	0 (0) 0	1 (0) 0	0 (0) 0
J Jenas	28 (1) 4	3 (0) 0	6 (0) 2	6 (1) 0
Y Kaboul	19 (2) 3	1 (0) 0	3 (1) 0	3 (0) 1
R Keane	32 (4) 15	3 (0) 2	4 (1) 2	7 (3) 4
L King	4 (0) 0	1 (0) 0	3 (0) 0	2 (0) 0
Y-P Lee	17 (1) 0	2 (0) 0	4 (0) 0	6 (0) 0
A Lennon	25 (4) 2	2 (1) 0	6 (0) 1	8 (1) 0
S Malbranque	35 (2) 4	3 (0) 0	5 (0) 2	9 (1) 1
J O'Hara	9 (8) 1	1 (1) 0	1 (1) 0	1 (3) 1
P Robinson	25 (0) 0	1 (0) 0	4 (0) 0	7 (0) 0
R Rocha	4 (1) 0	0 (0) 0	0 (0) 0	0 (0) 0
D Rose	0 (0) 0	0 (0) 0	0 (0) 0	0 (0) 0
W Routledge	1 (1) 0	0 (0) 0	0 (0) 0	0 (0) 0
P Stalteri	3 (0) 0	0 (1) 0	0 (0) 0	2 (1) 0
A Taarabt	0 (6) 0	0 (1) 0	0 (0) 0	0 (3) 0
T Tainio	6 (10) 0	2 (0) 0	2 (3) 0	2 (1) 0
J Woodgate	12 (0) 1	0 (0) 0	1 (0) 1	4 (0) 0
D Zokora	25 (3) 0	1 (0) 0	3 (1) 0	10 (0) 0

RESULTS 2007/08

11 Aug Sat	Away	Sunderland	Barclays Premier League	0-1	43967
14 Aug Tue	Home	Everton	Barclays Premier League	1-3	35716
18 Aug Sat	Home	Derby County	Barclays Premier League	4-0	35600
26 Aug Sun	Away	Man Utd	Barclays Premier League	0-1	75696
01 Sept Sat	Away	Fulham	Barclays Premier League	3-3	24007
15 Sept Sat	Home	Arsenal	Barclays Premier League	1-3	36053
20 Sept Thu	Home	Anorthosis Famagusta	UEFA Cup	6-1	35780
23 Sept Sun	Away	Bolton	Barclays Premier League	1-1	20308
26 Sept Wed	Home	Middlesbrough	Carling Cup	2-0	30084
01 Oct Mon	Home	Aston Villa	Barclays Premier League	4-4	36094
04 Oct Thu	Away	Anorthosis Famagusta	UEFA Cup	1-1	8000
07 Oct Sun	Away	Liverpool	Barclays Premier League	2-2	43986
22 Oct Mon	Away	Newcastle Utd	Barclays Premier League	1-3	51411
25 Oct Thu	Home	Getafe	UEFA Cup	1-2	26240
28 Oct Sun	Home	Blackburn	Barclays Premier League	1-2	36086
31 Oct Wed	Home	Blackpool	Carling Cup	2-0	32196
03 Nov Sat	Away	Middlesbrough	Barclays Premier League	1-1	25625
08 Nov Thu	Away	Hapoel Tel Aviv	UEFA Cup	2-0	10000
11 Nov Sun	Home	Wigan Athletic	Barclays Premier League	4-0	35504
25 Nov Sun	Away	West Ham	Barclays Premier League	1-1	34966
29 Nov Thu	Home	Aalborg	UEFA Cup	3-2	29758
02 Dec Sun	Home	Birmingham City	Barclays Premier League	2-3	35635
06 Dec Thu	Away	Anderlecht	UEFA Cup	1-1	22500
09 Dec Sun	Home	Man City	Barclays Premier League	2-1	35646
15 Dec Sat	Away	Portsmouth	Barclays Premier League	1-0	20520
18 Dec Tue	Away	Man City	Carling Cup	2-0	38564
22 Dec Sat	Away	Arsenal	Barclays Premier League	1-2	60087
26 Dec Wed	Home	Fulham	Barclays Premier League	5-1	36077
29 Dec Sat	Home	Reading	Barclays Premier League	6-4	36178
01 Jan Tue	Away	Aston Villa	Barclays Premier League	1-2	41609
05 Jan Sat	Home	Reading	FA Cup	2-2	35243
09 Jan Wed	Away	Arsenal	Carling Cup	1-1	53163
12 Jan Sat	Away	Chelsea	Barclays Premier League	0-2	41777
15 Jan Tue	Away	Reading	FA Cup	1-0	22130
19 Jan Sat	Home	Sunderland	Barclays Premier League	2-0	36070
22 Jan Tue	Home	Arsenal	Carling Cup	5-1	35979
27 Jan Sun	Away	Man Utd	FA Cup	1-3	75369
30 Jan Wed	Away	Everton	Barclays Premier League	0-0	35840
02 Feb Sat	Home	Man Utd	Barclays Premier League	1-1	36075
09 Feb Sat	Away	Derby County	Barclays Premier League	3-0	33058
14 Feb Thu	Away	Slavia Prague	UEFA Cup	2-1	11134
21 Feb Thu	Home	Slavia Prague	UEFA Cup	1-1	34224
24 Feb Sun	Wembley	Chelsea	Carling Cup	2-1	87630
01 Mar Sat	Away	Birmingham City	Barclays Premier League	1-4	26055
06 Mar Thu	Home	PSV Eindhoven	UEFA Cup	0-1	33259
09 Mar Sun	Home	West Ham	Barclays Premier League	4-0	36062
12 Mar Wed	Away	PSV Eindhoven	UEFA Cup	1-0	33000
16 Mar Sun	Away	Man City	Barclays Premier League	1-2	40188
19 Mar Wed	Home	Chelsea	Barclays Premier League	4-4	36178
22 Mar Sat	Home	Portsmouth	Barclays Premier League	2-0	35998
30 Mar Sun	Home	Newcastle Utd	Barclays Premier League	1-4	36067
05 Apr Sat	Away	Blackburn	Barclays Premier League	1-1	24592
12 Apr Sat	Home	Middlesbrough	Barclays Premier League	1-1	36092
19 Apr Sat	Away	Wigan Athletic	Barclays Premier League	1-1	18673
26 Apr Sat	Home	Bolton	Barclays Premier League	1-1	36176
03 May Sat	Away	Reading	Barclays Premier League	1-0	24125
11 May Sun	Home	Liverpool	Barclays Premier League	0-2	36063

MODRIĆ
14
LENNON
7

GW01608009
31
ELBA

Books in this series:

Fun to Play
Fun With Magic
My Fun to Cook Book
My Fun to Make Pictures Book
My Fun to Sew
My Fun With Wood Book
My Fun With Wool
My Fun With Yoga
My Learn to Cook Book
My Learn to Sew Book
My Learn to Swim Book
My Learn to Play Chess
My Learn to Play Football
My Learn to Ride Book

Acknowledgment
The Publishers wish to thank Waddingtons Playing Card Co Ltd for their kindness in supplying the cards for the illustrations.

Published 1975
by The Hamlyn Publishing Group Limited
London · New York · Sydney · Toronto
Astronaut House, Feltham, Middlesex, England

ISBN 0 600 33570 4
Printed by Litografia A. Romero, S.A.,
Santa Cruz de Tenerife, Canary Islands.
D. L. TF. 312 - 1975

My Fun to Play CARD GAMES

by George F. Hervey
illustrated by Tony Streek
photography by Philip James

HAMLYN
LONDON · NEW YORK · SYDNEY · TORONTO

Introduction

One of the best card players in England learnt to play bridge when he was only seven years old, and, while still at school, was able to tell men, twice his age, what they should have done and not done in games. This is rather like learning to swim by being thrown into the water at the deep end of a pool. Most of us prefer to start by stepping gingerly into the shallow end and working our way up to the deeper water. It is the same with card games. We need the experience and practice that simple games give us before we attempt to play a more advanced game like bridge.

MY FUN TO PLAY CARD GAMES has been written with this in mind. It will teach you what you need to know to play a variety of games, some more difficult than others. They have been divided into three main groups to satisfy everyone's taste – games of patience, competitive games and party games.

If you are by yourself and feeling bored, you can use this book to learn how to play a patience game; if you are having a party and want to have some fun with your friends, you might play a riotous game like Cheating or an old favourite like Snap or Old Maid; if you are in the mood for a more challenging game, one to make you think, there are plenty of competitive games to choose from.

Card games are meant to be enjoyed. You should not take a game of cards so seriously that you get no enjoyment from it; on the other hand, you should not treat a serious game so light-heartedly that you annoy the other players.

I hope that you will find in this book some games that appeal to you, and that you will enjoy playing them.

GEORGE F. HERVEY

Contents

Games of Patience. One-Pack Patiences

Games of patience are known in America as solitaires. It is a much better name for them because they are meant to be played by one player. Some are played competitively, but most are played as a welcome pastime for those recovering from an illness, or to relieve the boredom of a long train journey when looking out of a window loses its interest.

Most patience games are played with either one or two packs of cards. Unfortunately they take up a lot of room on the table, and you would be best advised to ask your father or mother to buy you two small packs of cards. Commonly known as patience packs, they are about half the size of the regular pack and are easier to play with.

Roll-Call

This is probably the simplest of all the many patience games and by playing it the beginner will get used to handling cards. The pack is shuffled and the cards are turned face upwards one at a time. As he turns the cards, the player says 'Ace', 'Two', 'Three', and so on up to 'King' and then starts again with 'Ace'. Whenever the card that is turned up corresponds with the number called, that card is put aside.

The game continues until all the cards have been put aside and the game is won, or until the cards keep coming up in the same order and the game is lost.

Leapfrog 1. Cards dealt in a row

Leapfrog 2. Cards in final order

Leap Frog

As you will have guessed, *Leap Frog* is a game in which the cards jump over each other. It is played with the ten pip cards of any one of the four suits. After shuffling they are dealt face upwards in a row on the table as shown in diagram 1.

The object of the game is to re-arrange the cards in five pairs (one card on top of another) so that the top cards of the pairs are in sequence from **A ◆** to **5 ◆**. In order to make a pair, a card may be moved either to the left or to the right and it must jump over two other cards which may be two single cards or one pair.

In the example shown, the **5 ◆** jumps over the **6 ◆** and **3 ◆** to the **7 ◆**; the **A ◆** jumps over the **8 ◆** and **4 ◆** to the **9 ◆**; the **4 ◆** jumps over the **8 ◆** and **10 ◆** to the **6 ◆**; the **2 ◆** jumps over the **A ◆–9 ◆** pair to the **8 ◆**; and the **3 ◆** jumps over the **4 ◆–6 ◆** pair to the **10 ◆**.

The cards are now in the order:

A ◆ 2 ◆ 3 ◆ 4 ◆ 5 ◆

with the **9 ◆** under the **A ◆**, the **8 ◆** under the **2 ◆**, the **10 ◆** under the **3 ◆**, the **6 ◆** under the **4 ◆**, and the **7 ◆** under the **5 ◆**. (See diagram 2.)

Tower of Hanoy

This is another interesting game tc play. It is played with nine cards: the Ace, Two, Three, Four, Five, Six, Seven, Eight and Nine of only one of the four suits.

These nine cards are shuffled together and dealt face upwards on the table in three rows. Suppose the original layout is as follows:

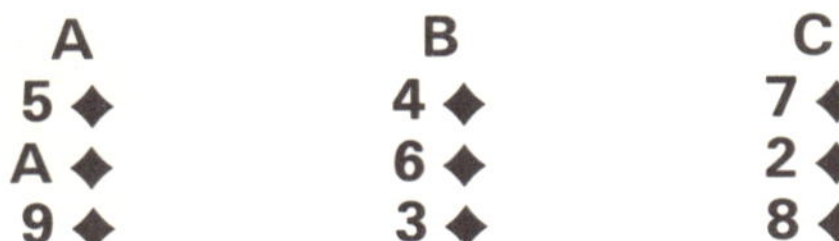

A	B	C
5 ◆	4 ◆	7 ◆
A ◆	6 ◆	2 ◆
9 ◆	3 ◆	8 ◆

The object of the game is to arrange the cards in one column with the Nine at the top, in downward sequence to the Ace.

The following four rules govern the movement of the cards:

1. Only one card may be moved at a time.
2. Only the bottom card of a column may be moved.
3. A card may be moved only to the foot of another column, and then only below a card that is higher in rank to it.
4. When any column is void of cards, a new column may be started by moving the bottom card of either of the two other columns to form the top card of the new column.

The skilful player will aim to get the **9** ◆ at the top of a column as quickly as possible, and the game will begin like this: move the **3** ◆ below the **9** ◆, the **6** ◆ below the **8** ◆, the 4 ◆ below the **6** ◆, and the **3** ◆ below the **4** ◆. Now the layout is:

A	B	C
5 ◆		7 ◆
A ◆		2 ◆
9 ◆		8 ◆
		6 ◆
		4 ◆
		3 ◆

and the **9** ◆ may be moved to the top of column B. The next step is to get the **8** ◆ below the **9** ◆, the **7** ◆ below the **8** ◆, and so on. It is not so easy, but, given time, the player is bound to succeed. The **A** ◆ is moved below the **9** ◆, the **3** ◆ below the **5** ◆, the **A** ◆ below the **3** ◆, the **4** ◆ below the **9** ◆, and the **A** ◆ below the **4** ◆. You will see the idea. Continue in this way until all the cards are in one column.

Try playing this game on your suitcase in the aeroplane or railway carriage on your way home from your holiday. It's great fun and you'll drive the other passengers mad trying to work out the moves.

Puss in the Corner

This game is one of the simplest of the one-pack building-up patiences. The four Aces are removed from the pack and placed face upwards in a square on the table. Suppose that the layout of cards is as follows (see diagram 1):

The Aces serve as foundations, to be built on in ascending colour-sequences (not necessarily suit-sequences) to the Kings. The rest of the pack is dealt one card at a time and the cards played to waste-heaps at the four corners of the square. When 4 cards have been dealt, make a pause and move any cards from the waste-heaps to the foundations. In the example shown, the **2♦** may be played to either the **A♦** or the **A♥**. Only the top card of each waste-heap is available for play.

When a 7 is turned up you may move any waste-heap on to another, and, having done so, may place either of the two remaining waste-heaps on the other.

When playing on a waste-heap you should try and place a card on a higher rather than on a lower one. If this proves impractical, you should play a card to a waste-heap that does not contain another card of the same rank. Most important of all is to avoid burying all four cards of one rank under higher cards.

If the game fails to come out in one deal, a second deal (but no more) is allowed. The four waste-heaps are picked up in any order and re-dealt without shuffling or mixing them together.

1. Puss in the Corner

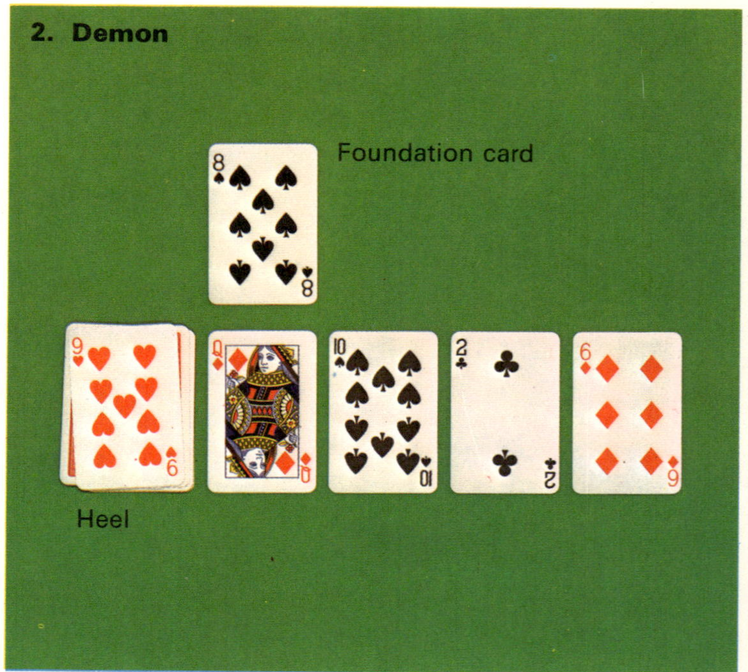

2. Demon

Demon (Canfield)

The *Demon* is known in America as the *Canfield,* because it is said to have been invented by Richard A. Canfield, a well-known card player of the late nineteenth century. At all events, it is a patience that everyone should know because it is generally thought to be one of the best, if not the best, of the many one-pack patience games.

Thirteen cards are dealt face downwards in a pile as a heel, and the top card is turned face upwards. Four cards are dealt face upwards in a row to the right of the heel to form the heads of columns. The eighteenth card is dealt face upwards and placed immediately above the heads of columns. This card indicates the foundations, and, as they become available, the other three cards of the same rank are placed alongside it. Let us suppose that the cards are dealt out like this (see diagram 2):

	8♠			
9♥	Q♦	10♠	2♣	6♦

In the diagram, the 8 is the foundation card.

The object of the game is to build ascending, round-the-corner suit sequences on the four foundation cards.

The top card of the heel is the **9 ♥**. The four cards to the right of the heel are the heads of the columns. They are packed in descending sequences of alternate colour. Thus you could play either the **J ♠** or **J ♣** on the **Q ♦**, and continue with either red 10.

The bottom cards of the four columns are always available to be played to a foundation, as is the top card of the heel. So, in this example, the **9 ♥** may be played on the **10 ♠** leaving the next card in the heel exposed and available for play.

When a space occurs, because a whole column has been removed, it must be filled at once with the top card of the heel, and the next card of the heel is turned face upwards. When there are no cards left in the heel, spaces are filled from the waste-heap, but they need not be filled at once.

The rest of the pack (the stock) is turned in batches of 3 cards, to a waste-heap. The top card of the waste-heap is always available for play either to a foundation or a column. If, at the end of the stock, there are less than three cards, they are turned singly. The stock is dealt and redealt until the game is either won by all four foundations being built up, or lost because no further move can be made.

It is by no means an easy patience, but it is a very fascinating one. You will enjoy playing it. It is estimated that you have only 1 chance in 30 of winning the game. You can improve the chances (that is to say, make the patience easier) by dealing 13 cards to the heel in a column, so that all can be seen, instead of in a pile with only the top card exposed; by not filling a space when it becomes vacant, but by leaving it open until a suitable card comes to light; and by transferring a part-sequence (not necessarily a complete sequence) from one column to another.

Two-Pack Patiences

A two-pack patience game is usually more difficult than a one-pack game. This is only natural because one has twice the number of cards to control. In general, two-pack patiences are more intricate and more interesting to play but some have the disadvantage of taking up a lot of room on a table.

Royal Parade

One of the best of the many two-pack games is *Royal Parade.* It is not difficult and the layout is rather an attractive one.

Two packs are shuffled together and 24 cards are dealt face upwards in three rows of 8 cards each.

The first step is to remove any Aces that may occur in the layout. They take no part in the game.

The second step is to arrange the cards in the layout so that the top row consists of the eight 2s, the middle row of the eight 3s, and the bottom row of the eight 4s.

The third step is to build up on these cards, following suit – the 5s, 8s and Knaves on the 2s; the 6s, 9s and Queens on the 3s; and the 7s, 10s and Kings on the 4s. Building up may be done only on a card in its proper row in the layout.

Suppose the cards are laid out as shown below.

Now, the **A♠** in the top row and the **A♦** in the middle row are removed. The **3♠** in the top row is moved to the space left vacant by the **A♦**, and the **2♣** in the middle row to the space left vacant by the **3♠**. The **2♠** in the middle row is moved to the space left vacant by the **A♠**, and the **3♣** in the top row to the space left vacant by the **2♣**. The **5♠** in the bottom row is built on the **2♠** in the top row, and the **8♠** in the top row is built on the **5♠**. Continue like this. You will see the idea.

When all moves have been made the player deals 8 cards from the stock playing them face upwards in a row to make waste-heaps below the layout. Any Aces that are dealt are removed. The player builds up on the cards, or fills spaces in the layout, with cards from the waste-heaps. When all the moves have been made another 8 cards are dealt from the stock to the waste-heaps, to cover the previous deal. Only the top cards of the waste-heaps may be moved to the layout.

The game ends when the stock is exhausted and no further moves can be made. If the game is won, the top row will show the eight Knaves, the middle row the eight Queens, and the bottom row the eight Kings. It looks like a parade of soldiers.

Royal Parade

Sultan (Emperor of Germany)

This is another two-pack patience that is not difficult and has an attractive layout.

Remove the eight Kings and one Ace of Hearts from the packs, and arrange them as shown in the illustration. Shuffle the packs together, and deal 4 cards face upwards to both sides of the centre (see diagram).

The object of the game is to build on the centre (except on the King of Hearts in the middle) ascending suit-sequences up to the eight Queens.

So, in this example, the **2 ♥** will be built on the **A ♥**, and the **A ♠** on one of the **K ♠**. The suit-sequences on the seven Kings are continuous, so that the Ace follows on the King. The spaces left vacant by playing these 3 cards to the centre are filled with the top cards from the stock.

The stock is dealt one card at a time, and if a card cannot be played to a sequence in the centre, or is not needed to fill a space, it is played to a waste-heap. The 8 side-cards are not built on.

When the stock is exhausted the cards in the waste-heap are shuffled and dealt a second time, and a third time if necessary, but no more.

The game is won when the King of Hearts in the centre is surrounded by the eight Queens. And so, you see that Sultan is a good name for it, but why it has been given the alternative name of *Emperor of Germany*, I do not know.

Sultan

Competitive Games

The games described in this section are sometimes called social games. Except for one game, they are contests of skill, sometimes played all against all and sometimes in partnerships. But, the playing of the game is always more important than the winning or losing of it. At all games, but particularly at card games, it is very important to be able to win without gloating and lose with good grace.

The general rules that have been laid down by custom for all card games are set out here.

Partnerships

In a partnership game, partners are decided by spread-eagling a pack face downwards on the table. Every player draws a card from the pack and turns it face upwards. The two who draw the highest cards play as partners against the other two as partners. If two or more players draw cards of equal rank they draw again.

Shuffling

Before dealing, the pack must be shuffled. Any player may shuffle, but the dealer has the right to have the final shuffle.

Cutting

After the pack has been shuffled it must be cut. The dealer passes the pack to his right-hand neighbour, who lifts some cards (at least five) off the top of the pack and places them alongside the rest of the pack. The dealer completes the cut by placing the bottom part of the pack on top of the other part.

Dealing

In a partnership game, the player who draws the highest card has first deal. In a game in which the players are playing all against all, the first deal may be determined by dealing a card face upwards to each player in turn; the one who is first to be dealt a Knave deals first. The dealer gives the top card of the pack face downwards to the nearest player on his left, the second card to the next player on the left, and so on until all the cards have been dealt. When a deal passes from player to player, it goes *in rotation* to the left, in the same clockwise direction as the dealing of the cards.

These rules should be observed. It is just as easy to do things correctly as incorrectly, and much more satisfactory. Doing things incorrectly ends in a muddle.

Games for Two Players

Pitch and Patience is one of the simplest of all card games, and good for beginners because there is no skill in it at all. Doing well at the game is all a matter of luck, and so the winner cannot gloat by saying, 'I won, therefore I play better than you.'

Pitch and Patience

The pack is placed face downwards on the table between the players and the top card is taken and placed face upwards alongside it. Each player in turn, beginning with the non-dealer, draws a card from the pack and aims to build upwards or downwards on the exposed card. That is to say, if the exposed card is an 8, he may play on it a 9 or a 7. On a King he may play an Ace or a Queen, on an Ace a 2 or a King, and so on.

If a player cannot play the card that he draws he retains it in his hand. The game ends when there are no more cards to be drawn from the pack and the winner is the person who holds in his hand the fewer cards.

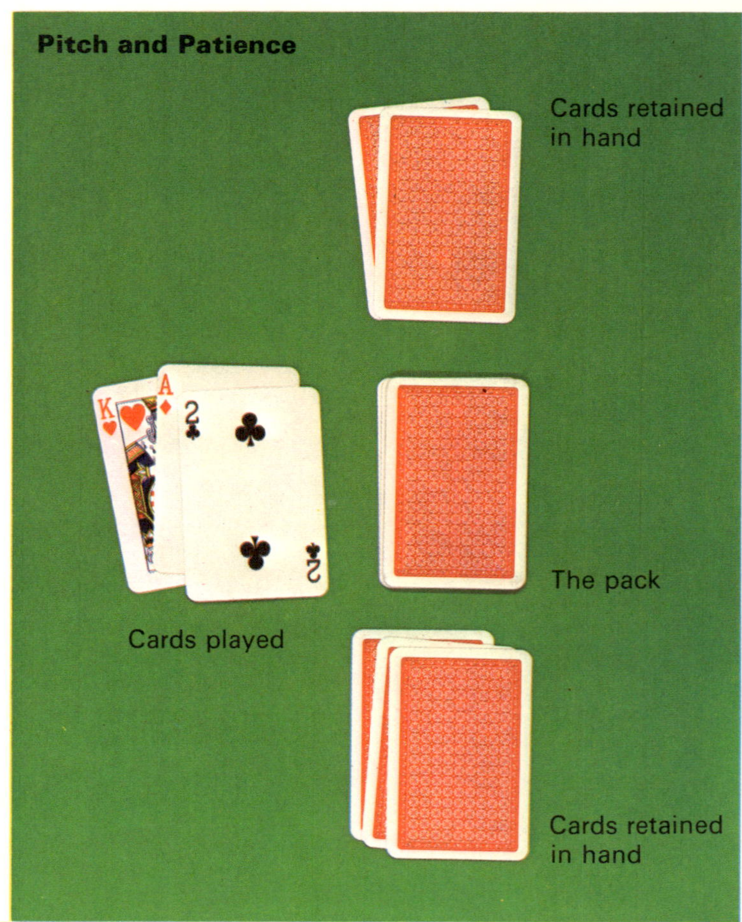

California Jack

This game is played with the full pack of 52 cards, the Ace ranking high and the 2 low.

The non-dealer cuts the pack and exposes the bottom card of it to determine the trump suit. The dealer then deals 6 cards to each player, and places the rest of the pack (the stock) face upwards on the table, being careful to square up the pack so that only the top card can be seen.

The non-dealer leads to the first trick. If he can, a player must follow suit to the card led; if he cannot, he may discard or win the trick by trumping it. If a player revokes he loses 1 point. The winner of a trick takes the top card of the stock and leads to the next trick. The loser of a trick takes the next card of the stock.

When there are no cards left in the stock, the last 6 cards are played out, and the tricks won by each player are looked at: 1 point is scored for winning the Ace of trumps (High), the 2 of trumps (Low), and the Knave of the trump suit (Knave), and the majority of points (Game) is determined by counting each Ace as 4 points, each King as 3 points, each Queen as 2 points, each Knave as 1 point, and each Ten as 10 points.

The game is won by the player who is first to score 10 points.

The hand shown in the diagram is a good one as it contains 2 cards (**A ♠** and **K ♦**) for winning tricks, and 3 cards (**4 ♣**, **2 ♠** and **2 ♥**) for losing them. A player should aim to keep winning *and* losing cards in his hand because if the exposed card of the stock is valuable he will want to win it, but if it is not, he will want to lose the trick on the chance that the next card of the stock will be a more valuable one. The Tens, of course, are the cards to go for.

The game is sometimes played with the stock placed face downwards on the table. It is less skilful as the winner of a trick does not know what card he will draw.

A good California Jack hand

Comet

For the game of *Comet* you will need two packs of cards with the same design on their backs. The packs must be prepared by throwing out all the Aces, putting all the red cards into one pack, all the black cards into another, and interchanging a red and a black 9. The packs are used alternately.

Eighteen cards are dealt to each player, and the remaining 12 are put aside – along with the Aces, they take no part in the game. The non-dealer begins the game by playing one of his cards face upwards to the centre of the table. One after the other the players build up on it by rank only. Suits are disregarded. Any number of cards, as long as they are of the proper rank, may be played in one turn. The four 6s, for example, may be played on a 5, the four Queens on a Knave, and so on. When a player is unable to build his turn ends (it is a stop) and his opponent begins another sequence by playing any card he chooses. Obviously, a King is always a stop as it is the highest card of a suit.

The 9 of the opposite colour is known as the comet. It may represent any card that the holder wishes, but may be played only in turn. It is a stop, and the player who plays it begins a new sequence.

The player who is first to get rid of all the cards in his hand is the winner. He scores the total of pips left in his opponent's hand, the King, Queen and Knave counting as 10 each. If both players are stopped and both are left with cards in their hands, both hands are counted. The lower hand wins and scores the value of the opponent's hand less the value of his own. If a player wins the hand while the comet is in the hand of his opponent he scores double. If a player wins by playing the comet, he doubles his score, and if he wins the hand by playing the comet as a 9 he quadruples his score.

German Whist

German Whist is a simple game but is interesting to play, and helps to train the memory for more advanced games.

Each player is dealt 13 cards, and the remaining 26 cards (the stock) are placed face downwards on the table between the players. The top card is turned face upwards to show which is the trump suit.

The non-dealer leads to the first trick. If he can, a player must follow suit to the card led; if he cannot he may either discard or win the trick by trumping it. The winner of a trick takes the top card of the stock into his hand; the loser takes the next card of the stock (without showing it to his opponent) and turns face upwards the next card of the stock.

After the first trick, the winner of a trick leads to the next.

When there are no more cards in the stock, the thirteen cards in the players' hands are played out. The player who wins most tricks receives an agreed number of points per trick for all in excess of those won by his opponent. That is to say, if the agreed number of points per trick is 5, and if Albert wins 16 tricks and Betty 10, then Albert scores 5×(16−10) = 30 points.

If you hold good cards in the trump suit, you should lead them early so that later in the game you will have control over your opponent. If the exposed card is a trump it is good play to try and win it. But, it is not always good play to win a trick. For example, suppose the exposed card is the **8♣** and Albert leads the **6♣**. Betty holds **♣Q.4.3.** It is not worthwhile wasting a Queen to win an 8, and it is better to play the **3♣**, keeping the **Q♣** for later in the game. Of course, if the exposed card was the **K♣** or **J♣** Betty would be right to win with the **Q♣** because then she would be exchanging the **Q♣** for an equivalent card and adding a trick to her total.

It is good play to hold control of as many suits as possible, because then you can win a trick, if the exposed card is valuable, without losing control of the suit.

In general, the game is a good test of memory.

German Whist

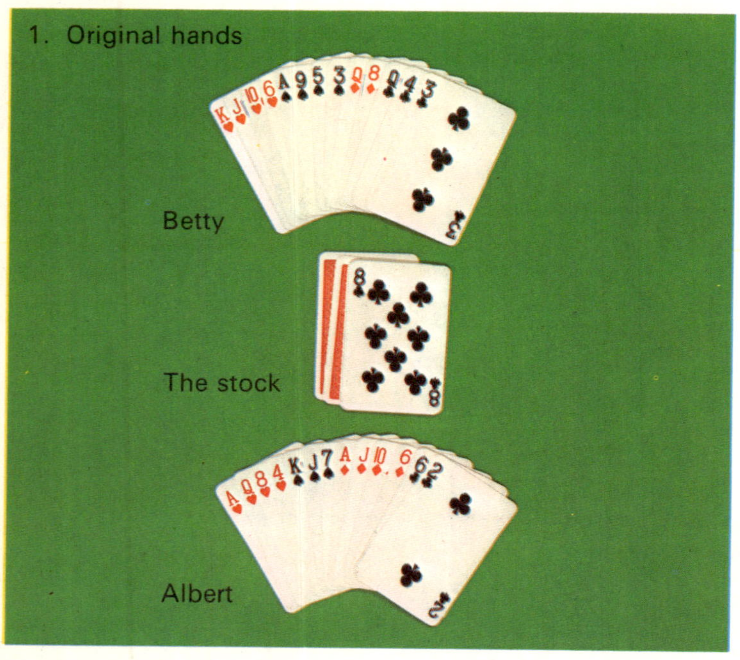

Tablanette

Many card games have come from Russia: *Tablanette* is said to be one of these.

Six cards are dealt to each player, and 4 cards face upwards to the table between them. If any Knaves are dealt to the table they are taken up and placed at the bottom of the pack and their spaces are filled with cards from the top of the pack. The pack is then put aside for a while.

The non-dealer plays first. If he plays a card of the same rank as any of the 4 cards on the table, he takes that card; or if there are 2 or 3 cards on the table whose values add up to that of the card played, he takes these cards. He may be able to do both. For the purpose of taking a card from the table, a King counts 14, a Queen 13, and an Ace 11 or 1. Other cards count at their pip values. The Knave plays a special part in the game: this will be explained later.

Suppose that the cards on the table are as shown in diagram 1.

Now, if the next player plays a King, he will take the **K ♣**; if he plays a Queen he will take the **9 ♦** and **4 ♥** as they total 13 (the value of a Queen); or if he plays a 7 he will take the **4 ♥** and **3 ♠** as they total 7.

The card played and those taken from the table are kept in a pile face downwards by the player who took them.

The players play in turn, and if a player has to play a card that does not permit him to take a card from the table, it is left on the table. If a player is able to take all the cards on the table (there may be only one or more than four) he announces 'Tablanette' and scores the total value of all the cards taken as well as the value of the card he has played.

Suppose the cards on the table are as shown in diagram 2.

Albert, whose turn it is to play, holds in his hand the cards shown in diagram 3.

He may announce 'Tablanette,' play the **Q ♥** and take up all the cards on the table, because his **Q ♥** takes the **Q ♦**; also the **2 ♠**, **4 ♥** and **7 ♣**, because they add up to 13, the value of a Queen. For this he will score 39 points – 13 for the **Q ♥**, 13 for the **Q ♦**, and 13 for the **2 ♠**, **4 ♥** and **7 ♣**.

The Knave has a special use – playing it allows the player to take all the cards on the table, but he does not score for tablanette.

When the players have played their 6 cards, the dealer deals another batch of 6 cards to each, and so on until all the cards in the pack have been dealt.

When the last deal has been played, any cards left on the table are taken by the player who last took a card from the table.

The players then score for the cards they have taken: 1 point for the **2 ♣** and for every Ace, King, Queen and 10, except for the **10 ♦** which scores 2 points; and the player who has taken the most cards scores a further 3 points.

The deal passes in rotation, and the game is won by the player who first reaches a total of 251 points.

Although Tablanette is primarily a game for two players, it may be played by three. It is played in exactly the same way except that the players are dealt four cards (instead of six) at each time.

1. Cards on the table

2. Cards on the table

3. Albert's hand

Games for Three Players

Games for three players are few and far between, and some are not very good. Knaves is thought to be one of the best, because it is not difficult and is good fun to play.

Knaves

Seventeen cards are dealt to each of the players, and the bottom card of the pack is turned face upwards to show which is the trump suit. It plays no other part in the game.

The player on the left of the dealer leads to the first trick. From then on, the player who wins a trick leads to the next. If he can, a player must follow suit to the card led; if he cannot he may either discard or play a trump. The trick is won by the player who plays the highest card of the suit led, or the highest trump.

For every trick that a player wins he scores 1 point, but 4 points are taken away from his score if he wins the Knave of Hearts, 3 points if he wins the Knave of Diamonds, 2 points if he wins the Knave of Clubs, and 1 point if he wins the Knave of Spades.

Unless a Knave is turned up as the last card, the total score for a hand is always 7 points: that is, 17 points for tricks less 10 points for winning Knaves.

The game is won by the player who is first to score 20 points.

Look at the diagram. Caroline deals. Therefore, Albert leads to the first trick. With these hands there should be some interesting play. Until the last Knave has been played, a player has to strike a balance between taking a trick (and so scoring a point) and the risk of being saddled with a Knave (and so losing points).

With all her trumps and high Diamonds, Betty seems to be in a position to score well. But, her hand is not really as good as it looks, because although the trumps and high Diamonds give her the advantage of winning tricks, she will also be forced to take Knaves. In fact, she will find it almost impossible to avoid winning the Knaves of Diamonds and Clubs, for a loss of 5 points. This is a big loss when the total score is only 7 points.

Black Maria

This game is similar to Knaves, as the players have to avoid taking tricks that contain certain cards (known as penalty cards), but it calls for rather more skilful play because the player has to pass cards to one opponent and receive some from another.

The 2 of Clubs is removed from the pack. It plays no part in the game. The remaining 51 cards are dealt, so that each player has 17 cards.

After a player has looked at his cards he passes any three of them to his right-hand opponent, and receives three from his left-hand opponent. He must not look at these until he has passed three on.

The player on the left of the dealer leads to the first trick. From then on, the player who wins a trick leads to the next. If he can, a player must follow suit to the card led; if he cannot he may discard any card he chooses. There is no trump suit, and the trick is won by he who plays the highest card of the suit led.

The object of the game is not to win tricks, but to avoid taking tricks that contain penalty cards. Altogether there are 16 penalty cards: all the Hearts (each of which counts 1 point against the player who takes the trick), the Ace of Spades (costing the winner of the trick 7 points), the King of Spades (costing 10 points), and the Queen of Spades or Black Maria (costing 13 points).

It is not a difficult game to play if you remember that it is not a matter of winning tricks but of avoiding taking tricks that contain penalty cards. Half the battle is knowing which cards are best to pass to your right-hand opponent. It is not always a good idea to pass on high cards. It is quite safe to keep them if they are supported by low cards. A good general rule is to try and get rid of all the cards of a suit (so that a penalty card can be discarded when the suit is led), and to try for a long suit containing low cards.

♥ A.K.7.4.3.2. ♦ Q.J.10.8.4.3. ♣ J.9. ♠ 6.5.3.

With a hand like this one, you would have nothing to fear in Hearts, and you would keep the Spades as support in case you were given a high card in the suit. You could not do better than pass on the two Clubs and the 10 of Diamonds in the hope that you might get a lower card in the suit, passed on by the opponent who is getting rid of all his Diamonds.

The play of the last few tricks is often very exciting.

Games for Four & More Players

The games described in this section are thought to be the most interesting of the competitive games. You will find that they are not difficult to play and you should not overlook them, because they are excellent stepping stones to more advanced games.

Most are played all against all, and if an odd number of players take part, they must be. If there is an even number of players, the games may be played either all against all or adapted for partnerships. As a start, it may be best to play in partnerships where this is possible – a game is easier if you have a partner to help you, rather than battling by yourself against all the other players. Either way, stick to one method.

Hearts

The game of *Hearts* has a number of variations and is the parent of Knaves and Black Maria (see pages 20 and 21) and Polignac and Slobberhannes (see page 23). In all these games you must try to avoid winning tricks that contain certain cards. In Hearts the penalty cards are all the cards of the Heart suit (each of which counts 1 point against the player, or partners, taking the trick) and the Queen of Spades (which costs the winner of the trick 13 points).

Although Hearts may be played by any reasonable number of players, it is at its best when played by four.

The player on the left of the dealer leads to the first trick. From then on, the player who wins a trick leads to the next.

If he can, a player must follow suit to the card led; otherwise he may discard any card. There is no trump suit, and the trick is won by the player who plays the highest card of the suit led.

Revoking is heavily penalised. The hand is abandoned and the player who has revoked (or his side in a partnership game), loses 26 points, as though he had taken all the penalty cards.

Polignac

This is sometimes played as a party game with the full pack of 52 cards. But it makes a better game if played by four with the short pack. This is a pack from which the 2s, 3s, 4s, 5s and 6s have been removed, so that it contains only 32 cards. Each player, therefore, receives 8 cards. The player on the left of the dealer leads to the first trick. From then on, the player who wins a trick leads to the next. There are no trumps and a trick is won by the player who plays the highest card of the suit led; if he can, a player must follow suit to the card led; if he cannot, he may discard any card he chooses.

The game is quite simple. All you have to do is to avoid winning a trick that contains a Knave. If the Knave of Spades (Polignac) is taken in a trick it costs the winner of the trick (or his side in a partnership game) 2 points; the other three Knaves cost the winners of the tricks 1 point each.

Polignac Trick containing the Knave of Spades

Slobberhannes

This is played in exactly the same way as Polignac, but points are lost differently. One point is lost by the players (or sides in a partnership game) who win the first trick, the last trick and the trick containing the Queen of Clubs. Another point is lost if all three tricks are won by the same player, or side in a partnership game.

The main interest in the game is in the general struggle to avoid winning the trick containing the Queen of Clubs.

Slobberhannes

Napoleon (Nap)

The game of *Napoleon* is always known as *Nap*. It is a game that everyone is expected to know because it is the simplest and easiest of the many trick-taking games.

Five cards are dealt to every player, so that as many as ten may take part. But, it is better if only five or six play because the game becomes rather dull when more than half the pack is in use.

In turn, every player (beginning with the player on the left of the dealer) has the choice of either passing or declaring to win a certain number of tricks in the ascending order of: Two, Three, Misery (an undertaking to win no tricks), Four, Nap (an undertaking to win all five tricks), and, if Nap has been called, Wellington (also an undertaking to win all five tricks, but at double points).

After the first call, every call must be higher than one that has already been made, and the player who has made the highest call leads to the first trick. The card that he leads determines the trump suit, but by previous arrangement a call of Misery may be played without a trump suit.

If he can, a player must follow suit to the card led; otherwise he may discard or trump. A trick is won by the player who plays the highest card of the suit led, or the highest trump, and the winner of a trick leads to the next.

Suppose that Eddie deals these cards:

Albert	Betty	Caroline	David	Eddie
♥ J.3.	♥ A.Q.	♥ none	♥ none	♥ none
♦ A.	♦ none	♦ K.J.10.9.	♦ none	♦ none
♣ 7.	♣ 9.4.	♣ none	♣ 10.6.3.2.	♣ A.K.Q.8.5.
♠ 4.	♠ 3.	♠ A.	♠ 6.	♠ none

Albert: 'Pass'.

Betty: 'Two'. It is very unlikely that she will be left to play the hand, and her call will force one of the others to call at least Three, which they may not be able to do. If, by chance, she is left to play the hand she will lead the Ace of Hearts and follow with the 3 of Spades hoping to win a second trick by trumping a Diamond or a Spade. There is also the chance that the King of Hearts is not in play, or that if it is, it will fall under the Ace.

Caroline: 'Three'. She expects to win two tricks in Diamonds (which she will make trumps by leading the King) and a trick with her Ace.

David: 'Misery'. If Misery is played with a trump suit he will lead the 6 of Spades.

Eddie: 'Nap'. Poor Eddie! With five trumps headed by the Ace, King and Queen, he has an almost certain Nap hand, but he will be beaten because David holds four Clubs headed by the 10. Bad luck, Eddie!

Points are scored only on the number of tricks declared. Tricks won above or lost below the number declared are ignored. Settlement is an even transaction:

Declaration	Declarer Wins	Declarer Loses
Two	2 points	2 points
Three	3 points	3 points
Misery	3 points	3 points
Four	4 points	4 points
Nap	10 points	5 points
Wellington	20 points	10 points

Scotch Whist (Catch the Ten)

One of the aims in *Scotch Whist* is to win the trick that contains the 10 of the trump suit. That is why the game is very often called *Catch the Ten*.

It may be played by any number up to eight, with the 36-card pack, that is a pack from which the 2s, 3s, 4s and 5s have been removed. The cards rank in the normal order from Ace (high) to 6 (low), except that the Knave of the trump suit is promoted above the Ace.

Every player must begin with the same number of cards. If five or seven are playing the 6 of Spades is removed from the pack; if eight are playing all four 6s are removed.

If an odd number take part, the game is played all against all, but if an even number take part they may play either all against all or in partnerships.

The dealer turns up the last card to indicate the trump suit, and the player on his left leads to the first trick. If he can, a player must follow suit to the card led; if he cannot he may either discard or trump. The player who plays the highest card of the suit led, or the highest trump, wins the trick, and leads to the next one.

The object of the game is to win the tricks that contain the 5 top trump cards. The player (or partnership) that does so scores 11 points for the Knave, 4 for the Ace, 3 for the King, 2 for the Queen and 10 for the Ten. On top of this, the players (or partnerships) count the number of cards won in the tricks they have taken and score 1 point for every card more than the number originally dealt to them.

The game ends when a player (or partnership) has won 41 points.

Scotch Whist The top trump cards (Hearts as trumps)

J	A	K	Q	10
11	4	3	2	10

Points scored

There is a lot of luck in the game – the 11 points for the Knave of the trump suit can be won only by the player to whom it has been dealt, and usually the luck of the deal decides who will win the tricks that contain the Ace, King and Queen. The card to go for is the 10 of the trump suit, and in a partnership game the player to whom it is dealt would do well to lead it if it is singleton or with only one other card of the suit. If his partner is able to win it with the Knave, his side will start with a big score, but if an opponent wins it the partnership must play to recover the lost ground by winning as many tricks as possible.

If the game is being played all against all, the player who has been dealt the 10 of the trump suit should play to get rid of all the cards of his shortest suit, so that he can win the 10 by trumping with it.

Blackout (Oh ! Well)

Blackout, sometimes called *Oh ! Well*, may be played by any number of players up to seven, but five, or perhaps six, makes the best number. As every player must start with the same number of cards, before a deal cards are taken out of the pack, and put aside without being looked at by the players. If five are playing, 2 cards are taken out of the pack; if six are playing, 4 cards are taken out; and if seven are playing, 3 cards are taken out. The cards are returned to the pack after the deal has been played, and fresh cards are taken out for the next deal.

The cards are dealt face downwards but the last card is turned face upwards to show which is the trump suit.

The player on the left of the dealer now announces how many tricks he thinks he will win; if he thinks that he will be unable to win a trick he says 'None'. Then every player in turn, clockwise, announces how many tricks he thinks he can win. These *declarations* as they are called, should be written down by one of the players (chosen before the game begins), who will also be in charge of recording the scores made by the players.

The player on the left of the dealer leads to the first trick. A player must follow suit if he can; otherwise he may discard or trump. The trick is won by he who plays the highest card of the suit led or the highest trump, and he leads to the next trick.

When all the cards have been played, the tricks won by the players are counted. A player who wins the exact number of tricks that he has declared scores 1 point for each and a bonus of 10 points. But, a player who wins more or less tricks than he declared scores only 1 point for each trick that he has won. A player who has declared 'None' scores 10 points if he does not win a trick.

The deal passes from player to player, and the game ends when one of them reaches a score of 100 points.

It is important to keep the tricks in an orderly way – so that they may be counted at the end of the deal – and at any time a player has the right to ask another how many tricks he has declared to win and how many he has already won. It is a point of honour that these questions should be asked only for one's own information and not to prompt the other players. If a player knows that he cannot possibly win the tricks that he has declared he must not tell the others.

It pays to be honest at this game. A player should declare the number of tricks that he thinks he can win, and play to win them – no more and no less. The beginner often falls into the trap of declaring 'None' as often as he can, in order to score the bonus of 10 points by losing every trick. In practice it is a losing game because the other players will combine to force him to win a trick. In much the same way, you must be careful when you have won the number of tricks that you have declared, because the others will be doing their best to deprive you of the bonus by forcing you to win another trick.

Blackout is a game of cut and thrust, and great fun to play.

Auction Pitch

This is an excellent game that is at its best when played by four, each playing for himself.

The game is played with the full pack of 52 cards, that rank in the order from Ace (high) to 2 (low) and the dealer gives 6 cards to each player in two bundles of 3.

The player on the left of the dealer bids first. Each player in turn may either make a bid or pass. A bid must be for at least 2 points, and for more than the preceding bid, except in the case of the dealer who may buy the hand for the same number of points as the preceding bid. The maximum number of points in a deal is 4, and the player who expects to win them bids 'Smudge'. The dealer cannot take this bid from him.

The successful bidder is known as *the maker*. He pitches (leads) to the first trick, and the card that he leads determines the trump suit. From then on, the player who wins a trick leads to the next.

If a player can, he must follow suit to the card led; if he cannot, he may either trump or discard. The winner of a trick is the one who plays the highest card of the suit led or the highest trump.

This is how to score:

High The player who holds the highest trump dealt scores 1 point.

Low The player who holds the lowest trump dealt scores 1 point.

Knave The player who wins the trick that contains the Knave of trumps (if it is in play) scores 1 point.

Game Counting the Ace as 4, the King as 3, the Queen as 2, the Knave as 1 and the Ten as 10, the player with the highest total in the tricks he has won scores 1 point. But, no-one scores the point if there is a tie.

Every player records what he scores, and if the maker fails to make his bid he is set back by the full amount of it. He records his score, and if it reduces him to a minus score, he puts a circle around it and is said to be *in the hole.*

The game is won by the player who first reaches 7 points, and if the maker and one or more of the others score 7 points in the same deal, the maker wins. As between the other three players, the points are counted in the order High, Low, Knave, Game.

A player who smudges and wins all 4 points, wins the game no matter what his score, unless he was in the hole when he smudged. If so, he wins only 4 points.

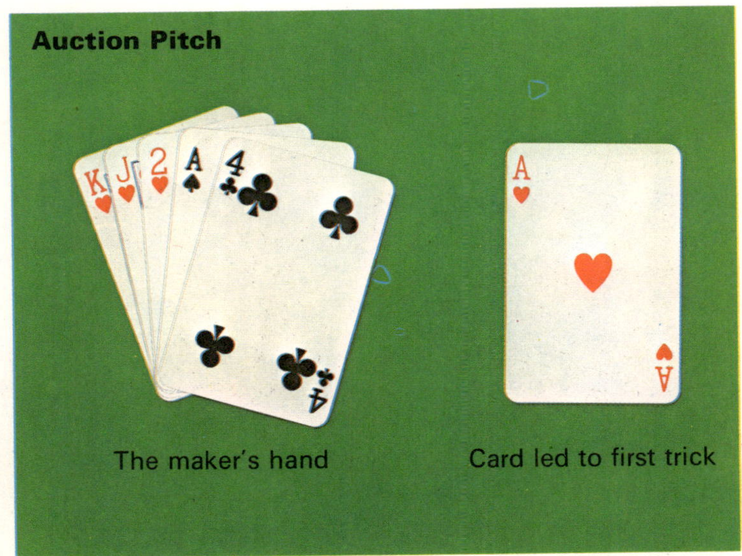

Auction Pitch

The maker's hand

Card led to first trick

Party Games

The games in this section are sometimes called *hilarious games*. It is quite a good name for them because parties are nothing without some fun and laughter, and the games that are best to play at parties are the ones that do not make you think too hard and depend mostly on luck. Nearly all the games that follow conform to these requirements, but Snap, one of the most elementary of games, is a notable exception: completely devoid of luck the result is decided by quickness, and Pelmanism, another simple game, calls for no more than a good memory, and makes a splendid training ground for more advanced games. Being able to concentrate is an advantage in any card game.

Beggar My Neighbour

This is a very old game, and a very simple one. It may be played by any number up to six.

The cards are dealt as far as they will go, because it does not matter if one or two players hold a card more than some of the others.

The players do not look at the cards dealt to them, but arrange them in a pile, face downwards, on the table in front of them.

The player on the left of the dealer then turns the top card of his pile face upwards and places it in the centre of the table; the player on his left places the top card of his pile face upwards on top of the card in the centre; and so on, round the table, until an Ace, King, Queen or Knave is turned up. When this happens the next player has to pay by placing on the pile 4 cards for an Ace, 3 for a King, 2 for a Queen and 1 for a Knave.

If, during the pay-off, an Ace, King, Queen or Knave is turned up, the player stops paying and himself is paid by the player on his left for the card turned up.

When a pay-off is completed the winner takes all the cards from the centre of the table and places them at the bottom of his pile.

The game is won by the player who collects all the fifty-two cards of the pack.

Donkey (Pig)

Donkey or *Pig* is another simple game that is best when played by six, but may be played by any number up to thirteen.

For each player in the game the 4 cards of one rank are kept, and the rest of the pack set aside. That is to say, if five players are in the game only the four Aces, four Kings, four Queens, four Knaves and four 10s are brought into play; if six are playing the four 9s are added; if seven the four 8s; and so on.

The cards are thoroughly shuffled and each player is dealt 4 cards. The object of the game is to collect 4 cards of one rank in your hand, or not to be the donkey or pig by being the last to notice when another player has.

After looking at his cards each player passes a card face downwards to the player on his left, and receives a card face downwards from the player on the right. He must not look at this until he has passed on his card.

When a player has collected 4 cards of the same rank, he stops passing and receiving cards, and puts his finger to his nose. He is the winner. The other players must also stop passing and receiving cards and put their fingers to their noses. The last one to do so is the donkey or pig, and when the game is being played by a fairly large number, it is surprising how long some take to notice that the game has been won and continue to pass and receive cards instead of putting their fingers to their noses.

Old Maid

This is a game that everyone knows, and a great favourite with children. It may be played by any number.

One of the Queens is removed from the pack and the rest of the cards are dealt out as far as they will go. It does not matter if some players have a card more than the others.

The players then discard from their hands, as pairs, any 2 cards of the same rank, and if a player has 3 cards of the same rank he discards two of them and retains the other. The dealer then offers his cards face downwards to the player on his left who draws a card from them. If he draws a card that pairs with one of his, he discards the pair; if not he mixes it with the cards in his hand. Either way, he offers his cards to the player on his left who draws a card from them. And so on, clockwise round the table until one player is left holding a solitary Queen – the Old Maid.

Let's suppose that six are playing, and the dealer has dealt himself the following cards (see below):

♥ K.8. ◆ K.Q.6.2. ♣ 6. ♠ 4.3.

He will pair off the **K ♥** and **K ◆**, and the **6 ◆** and **6 ♣**, leaving him with:

♥ 8. ◆ Q.2. ♠ 4.3.

He will shuffle these cards and offer them face downwards to the player on his left, doing his best, but not too obviously, to make him draw the **Q ◆**.

Old Maid

Dealer's original hand

Dealer's hand after pairing off

Ranter Go Round (Cuckoo)

Most card games, particularly party games, have more than one name. The Cornish game of *Ranter Go Round* is no exception; sometimes it is called *Cuckoo*.

It may be played by any number. Every player begins with three lives and the dealer gives one card to each.

The object of the game is to avoid being left with the lowest card, the King being high and the Ace low.

The game is begun by the player on the left of the dealer. He may either keep the card dealt to him or offer it to his left-hand neighbour with the command 'Change'. There is no choice, the player so commanded must exchange his card with his right-hand neighbour, unless he holds a King – then he announces 'King' and the game is continued by the player on his left.

When an exchange of cards has been made, the player who has been commanded to do so may pass on the card he has received in the same way; and so on, clockwise round the table, until the card is brought to a halt either by a King or by a player receiving a higher card in exchange for his, so that he has nothing to gain by passing it on.

Any player who is giving an Ace, a 2 or a 3 in obedience to the command 'Change' must announce the rank of the card.

The dealer is the last to play, and if he wishes to exchange his card he does so by cutting the remainder of the pack and taking the top card of the cut. If he draws a King he loses the hand, and with it one life. If he does not draw a King all the players expose their cards and the one with the lowest loses a life. If two or more tie for lowest card each loses a life.

When a player has lost his three lives he retires from the game. The others continue, until the game is won by the player who is left with at least one life.

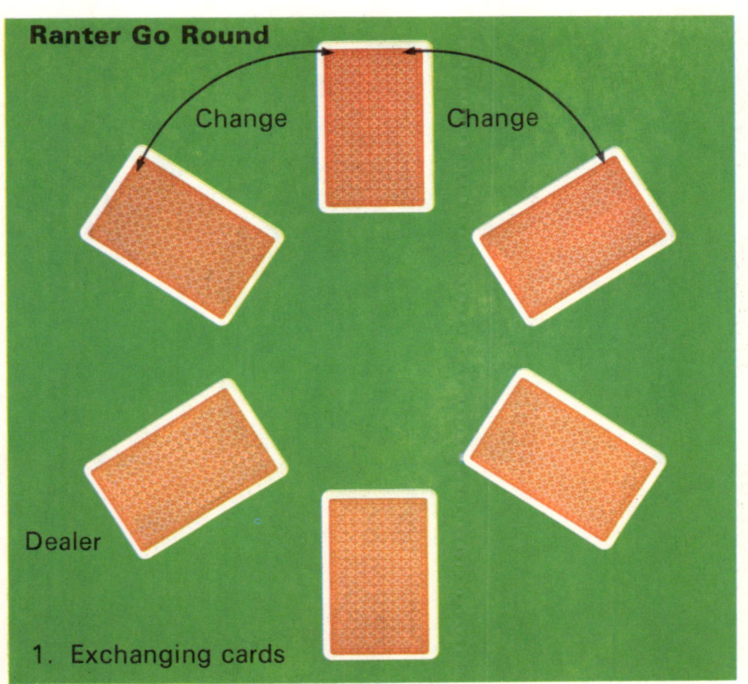

1. Exchanging cards

2. Dealer cuts remainder of the pack

Slapjack

This is a very easy game, and a rather riotous one that may be played by any number up to eight.

The cards are dealt as far as they will go, and it does not matter if some players have a card more than others. The players do not look at their cards but arrange them in a pile face downwards on the table in front of them.

The player on the left of the dealer begins the game by turning the top card of his pile face upwards and placing it in the centre of the table; the player on his left then turns face upwards the top card of his pile and places it on top of the one in the centre of the table; and so on, round and round the table.

Now, whenever a Knave is played to the centre of the table, the player who is first to slap his hand on it takes all the cards and places them at the bottom of his pile.

The game is won by the player who collects all 52 cards in this way.

If a player is left with no cards he may remain in the game until the next Knave is turned, and he may slap at it in an attempt to gain a new hand. But, if he fails, he is out of the game.

When a card is turned the player must turn it away from him so that he cannot see the face of the card before the others. The turn should be made as quickly as possible, so that the others cannot see the face of the card before the player who is turning it can.

Snap

Snap may be played by any number, but five makes the best game. If more than five take part two packs of cards, shuffled together, should be used.

The cards are dealt as far as they will go, and the players do not look at them but hold them face downwards in the palm of one hand.

The player on the left of the dealer begins the game by playing the top card from his hand face upwards to the table in front of him. The player on his left then does the same, and so on round the table. The played cards are built into a neat pile in front of each player, and only the top card of each pile should be visible.

Whenever two cards of the same rank are exposed, any player may call 'Snap' and the first to do so wins the two piles of cards and shuffles them into the cards left in his hand.

When a player has no more cards to turn, he remains in the game until he loses his pile.

The game is won by the player who collects all the fifty-two cards in the pack.

If a player calls 'Snap' and no two cards of the same rank are exposed, he gives each of the other players a card which they add to their own hands. If a player plays out of turn he must take the card back.

Animals (Menagerie)

Animals or *Menagerie* is played in much the same way as Snap, but before play begins the names of a number of animals are written on slips of paper and every player draws one from a hat.

The cards are dealt and played in the same way as at Snap, but when two cards of the same rank are exposed, the two players, instead of calling 'Snap', call out the name of the other player's animal three times. The player who calls first wins both piles.

As the names of some animals are easier to say than others, the selected names should all contain the same number of syllables – three for preference.

Albert	**Betty**	**Caroline**
(Buffalo)	(Marmoset)	(Guinea Pig)
♠ K	♦ 6	♥ 3

David	**Eddie**
(Kangaroo)	(Porcupine)
♦ 9	♣ 3

Caroline must now call: 'Porcupine, porcupine, porcupine' and Eddie: 'Guinea pig, guinea pig, guinea pig', and the first to do so takes both piles. Albert, Betty and David must not call, and if one of them does he forfeits one card to Caroline and one to Eddie.

Fan Tan

Fan Tan is known by several other names, but is not to be confused with the Chinese game of the same name.

It may be played by any number up to eight, with the full pack of 52 cards, the Kings being high, the Aces low.

The cards are dealt until the pack is exhausted, and the player on the left of the dealer begins the game by playing a 7 to the centre of the table. If he has no 7 the play passes to the player on his left, and so on.

When a 7 has been played, the next player must either play the 6 of the same suit to the left of it, the 8 of the same suit to the right of it, or a 7 of a different suit above or below it. The play continues clockwise round and round the table, the players building the suits up to the Kings on the right of the 7s, and down to the Aces on the left of them.

The hand is won by the player who is first to get rid of all his cards. He receives from each of the other players 1 point for every card that the player holds. The deal passes in clockwise rotation and the game is won by the player who is first to win an agreed number of points.

Look at the layout of cards shown below. The **9** ♣ should be played, as if another player plays the **10** ♣ the **J** ♣ can be played. It would not be a good idea to play the **4** ♦ as it gives another player the opportunity to play the **3** ♦.

Snip-Snap-Snorem

This game may be played by any number. The cards are dealt out as far as they will go, and the player on the left of the dealer plays any card he likes to the table. If the player on his left has a card of the same rank he plays it and says 'Snip'; if he hasn't he passes, and the next player either plays a card of the same rank or passes. Play continues clockwise round the table. The player of the third card of the same rank says 'Snap', and the player of the fourth card says 'Snorem'.

The player of the fourth card leads to the next round, and if any player holds more than one card of the same rank he plays them one after the other saying the appropriate words. A player must play a card if he can. If a 10 is led, a player with two 10s must play both and say 'Snip' and 'Snap'. He must not hold one back to make it a 'Snorem' card and gain the lead.

The game is won by the player who is first to get rid of all his cards.

The Earl of Coventry

This is played in much the same way as Snip-Snap-Snorem, but every time a card is played the player must recite a line of doggerel. The lines must scan, the rhyming word may not be repeated in any one verse, and the last line must include the words 'The Earl of Coventry'.

Suppose that six people are in the game and that Albert has the lead. He plays the 9 of Clubs:

Albert 9♣ 'I had a horse, a lordly cart-horse'
Betty Passes
Caroline 9♥ 'That fed on warm oats and slept on gorse'
David 9♦ 'Last week I sold him in remorse'
Eddie Passes
Fanny 9♠ 'To the Earl of Coventry, of course'

Difficult? Maybe, but have a go. It's lots of fun.

Authors

Authors is a simple game which is just right for five or six players.

The pack is dealt out as far as it will go and each player in turn, beginning with the one on the left of the dealer, asks another player to give him a certain card. He may ask for any card he likes so long as he himself holds a card of the same rank.

Let us suppose that five people are in a game and that one of them has been dealt the hand shown in the diagram. He will ask one of the other players to give him the 10 of Hearts, because he already holds the three other 10s, and the object of the game is to complete a trick of four cards of the same rank.

If the player who is asked for a card holds the right one he gives it to the asker, who continues by asking any player for another card. If the player asked has not got the card asked for, the privilege of asking passes to him.

When a player has collected four cards of the same rank he shows them and places them face downwards on the table in front of him as a trick. The winner of the game is the player who wins most tricks.

The game lends itself to a bit of low cunning, which makes it all the more fun to play. For example, it is not wrong to ask a player for a card that you yourself hold, in an attempt to put off another player who might spoil your hand by asking for this card.

Authors A player's hand

Go Fish

Go Fish is very similar to Authors but easier to play. It is suitable for four or five players and each is dealt five cards. The rest of the pack (it is called the stock) is placed face downwards in the centre of the table.

The player on the left of the dealer begins the game by asking one of the players to give him all the cards of a certain rank that he holds. He may ask for any rank so long as he holds at least one card of the same rank. The player must hand over all the cards of the specified rank that he holds, but if he holds none he says: 'Go fish'. The asker must then take the top card of the stock.

A player's turn to ask continues for as long as he receives the cards he asks for. If he has to fish, and he draws a card of the specified rank from the stock, he must show it before continuing to ask. If he fails to obtain a card of the specified rank, either from the player he has asked, or from the stock after being told to fish, the privilege of asking passes to the player on his left.

When a player obtains all four cards of a rank, he shows them and places them face downwards as a trick on the table in front of him.

The game ends when all thirteen tricks have been won, the winner being he who has won most tricks.

Cheating

This is an amusing and rather riotous game that may be played by any number. According to the number of players taking part, two, three or even four packs of cards are shuffled together and sufficient cards are removed so that every player begins with the same number of cards.

The player on the left of the dealer begins the game by placing a card face downwards in the centre of the table and saying 'Six' or any number he chooses. The next player places a card on top of it and says 'Seven', the next 'Eight' and so on up to 'King', when the next player says 'Ace', the next 'Two', the next 'Three', the next 'Four', and so on.

The feature of the game is that a player need not necessarily play the card he announces, and, of course, sometimes he is not able to. So when a player has announced that he has played a certain card, anyone may challenge him by saying 'Cheating'. The card is then exposed. If it is found that the player *has not* played the card he announced, he must take into his hand all the cards on the table; if he *has* played the card that he announced, the challenger must take all the cards on the table into his hand.

After a challenge, the player on the left of the challenger restarts the game by playing a card to the centre of the table and announcing it.

The game is won by the player who is first to get rid of all his cards.

I Doubt It

A variation of Cheating has been given the more polite name of *I Doubt It*. It may be played by any number up to twelve or thirteen, but if more than six take part two packs of cards, shuffled together, should be used.

The cards are dealt as far as they will go, and the game is begun by the player on the dealer's left. He puts face downwards on the table in front of him any number of cards from one to four (from one to eight if the double pack is in play) that he chooses, and announces that they are so many Aces. The player on his left then puts down any number of cards from one to four or eight, and announces that they are so many Kings; the player on his left does the same with Queens, and so on up to 2s, when the next player announces Aces, the next Kings, and so on.

The player need not necessarily put down the cards of the rank that he announces, and after a player has made an announcement any other player may challenge him by saying 'I doubt it'. When this challenge is made, the cards are turned face upwards. If it is found that he *has* put down the cards that he announced, the challenger must take into his hand these cards and all the other cards that have been played on the table. If it is found that the player *has not* put down the cards that he announced, he must take them back into his hand along with all the other cards that have been played on the table. If no-one challenges, the cards remain on the table, to be taken by someone later.

If more than one player challenges, the one who was first to do so is the official challenger, and if several players challenge simultaneously the one nearest to the player's left is the official challenger.

The game is won by the player who is first to get rid of his cards, and, as in Cheating, a little low cunning is not out of place – such as, complaining that you have none of the cards that it is your turn to play when, in fact, you have two or three of them and you play them resignedly.

Look at the example shown in the diagram. Six players are in the game and Fanny deals.

Albert is first to play. He decides to take a risk and announces two Aces, although he holds only one. As a rule it is best to tell the truth, but so early in the game a challenge is unlikely, and, if one is made Albert will not be saddled with a lot of cards. He must be careful to announce no more than two Aces, however. To announce more would almost certainly result in a challenge, because it is against the odds to be dealt three cards of the same rank. With the ♠ **A** Albert puts down the ♦ **K** and announces 'Two Aces'. He has done well to retain the ♣ **8** (as he will have to announce 8s next round) and the ♥ **2** and ♣ **2** (as he has to announce 2s on the third round). No-one challenges.

Betty puts down the ♣ **K** and ♠ **K** and announces 'Two Kings'. No-one challenges.

Caroline puts down the ♦ **Q** and announces 'One Queen'. No-one challenges.

David is becoming a bit impatient and decides to take a chance. Along with the ♣ **J** he puts down the ♥ **9** and announces 'Two Knaves'. Bad luck, David. Fanny knows differently. She gives David a pitying look and quickly says 'I doubt it'. David, therefore, has to take the two cards back into his hand, as well as those put down by Albert, Betty and Caroline. Maybe he'll get his own back when it is Fanny's turn to play. She has to put down 9s and she hasn't one. Meanwhile . . .

Eddie puts down the ♥ **10** and announces 'One Ten'. No-one challenges.

Fanny It is Fanny's turn to play and put down 9s. As she does not have any 9s, the fun begins.

Pelmanism

This is a very easy game suitable for any number of players. It calls for a large table because the dealer places at random all fifty-two cards face downwards on the table, no two cards touching each other, some at one angle others at another.

The object of the game is to make pairs consisting of two cards of the same rank, and the player who collects most pairs wins the game.

Beginning with the player on the left of the dealer, each player in turn faces any two cards. If they are a pair he keeps them as a trick and tries again. If they are not a pair he turns them back face downwards as nearly as possible in their original positions. The next player then has a go.

For the first two or three rounds it is a matter of guesswork, but as the game progresses anyone with a reasonably good memory will remember the positions of many of the cards that have been turned and not paired. By turning a card that has not already been turned a player gives himself a good chance to pair it.

Fourteens

This game is a variation of Pelmanism and is played in exactly the same way, except that the Kings are counted as 13, the Queens as 12, the Knaves as 11, and the other cards at their pip values; and, instead of pairing two cards of the same rank, the players pair 2 cards that total 14. This is to say the pairs are King and Ace, Queen and 2, Knave and 3, 10 and 4, 9 and 5, 8 and 6, 7 and 7. It makes a change if nothing more.

Newmarket

Newmarket is a modern variation of the old game of Pope Joan. It is suitable for any number of players up to eight, and is played with the full pack of 52 cards and an Ace, King, Queen and Knave (each of a different suit) from another pack. These 4 extra cards are known as *boodle cards*; they are placed face upwards in a row in the centre of the table.

Before the cards are dealt the dealer places two counters on each of the boodle cards and the other players place one counter on each.

The dealer deals the cards one at a time to each player and to an extra hand, known as the dummy-hand, which must not be looked at by any of the players. As the players must start with the same number of cards, any over-cards are dealt to the dummy-hand.

The cards rank from Ace (high) to 2 (low) and the player on the left of the dealer leads first. He may lead a card from any suit, but he must lead the lowest card that he holds of that suit. The players do not play in rotation. The next play is made by the player who holds the next higher card of the suit, and so on, until the run is stopped because either a player plays the Ace of the suit or the next higher card is in the dummy-hand. Either way, the player who played the last card begins a new run. He must lead the lowest card that he holds of a different suit, and if he holds no other suit, the lead passes to the player on his left.

When a player plays a card that is identical with one of the boodle cards, he wins all the counters that have been put on it.

The object of the game is not only to win the counters on the boodle cards but also to get rid of all one's cards, because the player who is first to do so receives a counter from each of the other players. If no player gets rid of all his cards, the one who is left with the fewest number of cards wins the hand, and if there is a tie between two or more players they divide the counters between them.

If a hand comes to an end before the counters on one or more of the boodle cards have been won (because the corresponding cards are in the dummy-hand), they are carried forward to the next deal.

Let us suppose that there are five players in the game. The boodle cards are:

♥ A   ♦ K   ♣ Q   ♠ J

and each will have six counters on it (see below).

Albert makes the first lead and plays the ♥ **9** because he hopes to win the counters on the ♥ **A** boodle card. David plays the ♥ **10**, Eddie the ♥ **J**, David the ♥ **Q** and Caroline the ♥ **K**. Albert, therefore, plays the ♥ **A** and wins the counters on the boodle card.

He now leads the ♦ **5**, on which Betty plays the ♦ **6**, Eddie the ♦ **7**, David the ♦ **8** and Albert the ♦ **9**. This is a stop because the ♦ **10** is in the dummy-hand. Albert, however, is well on the way to winning the hand because already he has got rid of four of his eight cards, and now he has the lead, can get rid of a fifth.

Albert leads the ♣ **2**, David plays the ♣ **3** and Eddie the ♣ **4**. This brings the run to a stop as the ♣ **5** is in the dummy-hand. Eddie, therefore, begins a fresh run, and chooses the ♠ **8** in the hope that the run will not be stopped before he can win the counters on the ♠ **J** boodle card.

And so on.

Newmarket

Albert

Betty

Caroline

Boodle cards

Eddie

Dummy hand

David

Thirty-One

This is an excellent party game because any number up to fifteen may take part, and it is very simple to play.

It is played with the full pack of 52 cards that rank in the order from Ace (high) to 2 (low).

Before the deal, everyone places an agreed number of counters into a pool. The dealer then deals, face downwards, 3 cards to each player, and 3 cards face upwards to the centre of the table. It is known as the *widow-hand.*

Now, beginning with the player on the left of the dealer, every player in turn must exchange one of his cards with a card in the widow-hand. He must not pass, and he is not allowed to exchange more than one card. Counting the Ace as 11, the King, Queen and Knave as 10 each, and the other cards at their pip values, the object of the game is to hold 3 cards of the same suit which will add up to 31. Next in value is a hand that consists of 3 cards of the same rank. Failing either, the pool is won by the player who holds the highest total in any one suit.

The exchange of cards with the widow-hand continues clockwise round the table until a player has obtained a 31-hand. When this occurs he shows his cards, claims the pool, and the deal passes. At any stage of the game, however, a player who thinks he has a hand good enough to win may rap the table. The other players, in turn, now have the right to stand pat with the cards that they hold, or exchange one more card with the widow-hand. The players then expose their cards and the one who holds the best hand wins the pool.

A player would be advised to rap the table if his hand totals 25 or more. It is quite a good hand that will win more times than it will lose.

Great Expectations

This game is particularly good for parties – it is amusing and as there is no skill in the game anyone can join in without previous explanation of how the game is played. It may be played by any number up to ten.

Each player begins with an agreed number of counters, and each is dealt an equal number of cards. The excess cards are put up to auction by the dealer, and a card is taken by the player who pays most counters for it.

The dealer now takes a second pack of cards. It is shuffled and cut, and the top five cards are placed face-downwards on the table.

The players now pay the dealer a stake as follows. Three players pay 8 counters each, four pay 6 counters each, six pay 4 counters each and eight pay 3 counters each. Five players pay 5 counters each, and eight, nine or ten players pay 3 counters each.

The dealer adds these counters to the ones he has received from auctioning the excess cards, and puts them on the backs of the five cards on the table. He must put at least 1 counter on a card.

The dealer now turns the cards in the remainder of the second pack, and as he does so he calls out each card. The player who holds the corresponding card puts it on the table in front of him.

When all 47 cards have been turned, the five cards on which the counters have been staked are faced one by one, and the players who hold the corresponding cards win the counters that have been staked on them.

Glossary

Boodle Cards In Newmarket, extra cards in a layout on which counters are placed.

Build In games of patience, to play a card of the same suit on the next above or below it in rank.

Colour-Sequence A sequence of all-red or all-black cards.

Court Card Any King, Queen and Knave; a picture card.

Declaration Naming a trump suit or game; the trump suit or game so named; a call; a bid.

Discard A card that is not of the same suit as the one led nor a trump; to play such a card.

Doubleton An original holding of two cards of a suit.

Dummy-Hand In Newmarket, an extra hand dealt to the table and not looked at by the players.

Fish To draw a card from the stock.

Follow Suit To play a card of the same suit as that of the card led.

Foundation In games of patience, a card on which a complete suit or sequence is built.

Heel In games of patience, cards placed aside in one or more packets for later use in the same deal.

In the Hole A minus score.

Layout Cards laid out on the table in a prescribed pattern.

Lead To play first to a trick; a card so played.

Maker In Auction Pitch, the player who decides the trump suit.

Misery (Misère) To contract not to win a trick; this contract.

Nap In Nap(oleon), a declaration to win all five tricks.

Penalty Card A card that if won in a trick loses points.

Pip Card A card whose rank is determined by the large suit symbols (♥ ♦ ♠ ♣) painted on it, excluding the index marks.

Pitch In Auction Pitch, the opening lead that determines the trump suit.

Pitcher In Auction Pitch, the player who makes the opening lead.

Rank The ordinal position of a card in its suit.

Revoke Failure to follow suit when able to, or to play a card as required by rules of correct procedure.

Rotation The progression of the turn to deal, to receive cards or to play which is normally clockwise.

Round A division of dealing or playing in which each player participates once.

Round-the-Corner-Sequence A sequence of cards in which the Ace follows after the King and before the 2.

Sequence Two or more cards of adjacent rank.

Short Pack A pack from which some of the cards have been removed before the deal.

Singleton An original holding of one card of a suit.

Smudge In Auction Pitch, a bid to win all four points.

Stand Pat To play with one's original hand; to decline to draw additional cards.

Stock The undealt part of the pack which may be used later.

Stop Interruption of play caused by the absence of the next card in sequence; the card so absent.

Suit Any of the four sets (Hearts, Diamonds, Spades, Clubs) into which a pack of cards is divided.

Suit-Sequence A sequence of cards all of the same suit.

Trick A round of cards during the play to which each active player has contributed one card; the packet of such cards when gathered.

Trump A card of the trump suit; to play such a card.

Trump Suit The suit selected by the rules of the game to have the privilege that every card of it ranks higher than any card in the other three suits.

Turn-Up A card turned face upwards after the deal in order to determine the trump suit.

Void Absence of every card of a suit from the hand.

Waste-Heap In games of patience, cards put aside as unwanted or unplayable; a pile of discards.

Widow-Hand Extra cards dealt to the table at the same time as the hands are dealt to the players.

Index of Games

To the
Castle
To the
Menagerie